Proposals and Realizations

Published by Kunstverein Publishing, Grazer Kunstverein, and Sternberg Press

Editor: Kari Conte
Publication manager: Krist Gruijthuijsen
Copyeditor: Max Bach
Proofreading: Niamh Dunphy
Lithography: Carsten Humme
Design: Marc Hollenstein, Amsterdam
Printing: Pöge Druck, Leipzig
Edition: 1,500

ISBN 978-3-943365-93-1

Every effort has been made to obtain copyright permission for images.
Any inadvertent omissions will be corrected in future editions.

Published in collaboration with:

Arnolfini
16 Narrow Quay
Bristol BS1 4QA
United Kingdom
www.arnolfini.org.uk

Institute of Modern Art
Judith Wright Centre for Contemporary Arts
420 Brunswick St. Fortitude Valley
PO Box 2176, Fortitude Valley BC QLD 4006
Brisbane
Australia
www.ima.org.aus

Marabouparken
Löfströmsvägen 8
172 66 Sundbyberg
Sweden
www.marabouparken.se

With generous support from:
Graham Foundation, Chicago
Ronald Feldman Fine Arts, New York

With thanks to:
Felisia Tandiono, Photographic Archivist
Varvara Mikushkina, Former Media Archivist, Ronald Feldman Fine Arts
Victoria Dejaco, Curatorial Assistance, Grazer Kunstverein
Jenny A. A. Korns, Archival Assistant, Mierle Laderman Ukeles Office
Maxine Kopsa, Founder, Kunstverein Publishing

Kunstverein Publishing
Gerard Doustraat 132
1073 VX Amsterdam
The Netherlands
www.kunstverein.nl

Grazer Kunstverein
Palais Trauttmansdorff
Burggasse 4
8010 Graz
Austria
www.grazerkunstverein.org

Sternberg Press
Caroline Schneider
Karl-Marx-Allee 78
D-10243 Berlin
www.sternberg-press.com

MIERLE LADERMAN UKELES

SEVEN WORK BALLETS

CONTENTS

PREFACE

Mierle is a mother. A concerned one. I would say that she is the mother of all mothers.

In 1969, following the birth of her first child, she wrote "Manifesto for Maintenance Art" as a challenge to the opposing binaries that draw the line between art/life, nature/culture, and public/private. "I am an artist. I am a woman. I am a wife. I am a mother. (Random order). I do a hell of a lot of washing, cleaning, cooking, renewing, supporting, preserving, etc. Also, (up to now separately) I 'do' Art. Now I will simply do these everyday things, and flush them up to consciousness, exhibit them, as Art." These legendary words have defined and shaped a body of work that started off quite literally in the kitchen and ended up in a large office located inside the New York City Department of Sanitation. Maintaining one's life and its environment, and acknowledging those that do so, has become Mierle's opus.

Having completed a series of performances that formalized and emphasized her ideas around maintenance, both personal and institutional, in 1977 she created an unsalaried position as Artist-in-Residence with the New York City Department of Sanitation. She proposed to do work that would incorporate dialogue and community participation around everyday issues, land degradation, and ecological sustainability. *Touch Sanitation* (1977), her first project as Artist-in-Residence for the New York City Department of Sanitation, drew attention to the maintenance of urban ecological systems in general and the misrepresentation of sanitation workers in particular. She traveled to each sanitation district of New York City to shake the hands of over 8,500 sanitation workers during this yearlong performance, to thank every worker individually for, as she said to each one, "keeping New York City alive."

After watching the 1977 St. Patrick's Day Parade, Mierle noticed how sanitation work was largely ignored, and wrote a proposal to turn it into a spectacle in the form of a three-part performative endeavor, which was realized five years later. *Sanitation Celebrations* (1983)—in particular its second movement, *Ballet Mécanique for Six Mechanical Sweepers*— was the starting point for her ongoing series of work ballet performances, which activate socio-urban choreographies of workers, trucks, barges, and hun-

dreds of tons of recyclables in cities across the globe. The ballets operate on a speculative level on which human and mechanical labor merges. Even though the intention of each ballet differs, the performances resemble those of Futurism, in which fusions between man and machine were first explored on a performative level. Mierle's interests, however, do not lie in the mechanistic, dehumanized aspect, but rather in life and its preservation. Just like in many of her other works, these work ballets function as a way of making the invisible visible by using art as an agent for possible change.

This publication functions as a way to draw attention to a specific body of work within the larger scope of the artist's unique and pioneering voice that has inspired so many. It would have never come to completion without the great dedication, effort, and dialogue between editor Kari Conte and Mierle Laderman Ukeles. On behalf of Kunstverein in Amsterdam, Grazer Kunstverein, Arnolfini, Institute of Modern Art, and Marabouparken, I would like to thank Marc Hollenstein for the design, the Graham Foundation in Chicago, and everyone at Ronald Feldman Fine Arts in New York, especially Ronald and Frayda Feldman and Marco Nocella, for their support.

Krist Gruijthuijsen
Artistic Director, Grazer Kunstverein

THE BALLET BOOK: CHOREOGRAPHY AND LABOR

KARI CONTE

In 2012 hundreds of audience members in Tokamachi stood under the fierce Japanese summer sun in a grassy field that functioned as an open-air theater. Two immense tire dozers, which clear meters of snow in the winter, were now performing their reprised roles of Romeo and Juliet, and moved closer to kiss each other's gleaming peach-and-purple-colored blades. This moment was preceded and followed by an ensemble of thirteen snow vehicles—at once delicate and strong—dancing in and out of unison, in a collaboratively choreographed flow of space and time. At the end of the hour-long dance of the rotaries, tire dozers, and motor grader, the audience rushed to the vehicles in sheer appreciation of the drivers' dexterity in the work ballet.

What the audience didn't see was how this performance, in certain ways, was a decade in the making. Mierle Laderman Ukeles had originated the first *Snow Workers' Ballet* in 2003 for Tokamachi and the Echigo-Tsumari Triennial. While developing this first ballet, and subsequently for the second iteration in 2012, Ukeles immersed herself in the infrastructure and culture of the city, notable for its vast agriculture and Japan's longest river, with an aging population typical in much of Japan; not surprisingly, the triennial was founded to bring renewed interest and activity to the region. Solidarity between Ukeles and the drivers was built up over weeks of planning and creating the work ballet together, starting from a set of straightforward but complex questions: What can you do? What have you always thought about doing? From these questions emerged a work ballet rooted in narrative, and built from trust between Ukeles and the drivers, some of whom had participated in the ballet a decade earlier.

The two work ballets for the Echigo-Tsumari Triennial were the last of seven large-scale collaborative performances involving workers, trucks, barges, and hundreds of tons of recyclables and steel, the first two taking place in 1983 and 1984 in New York City, and then in Rotterdam, Pittsburgh, Givors, and Tokamachi. Using the expanded urban-scape as site and context, each work ballet took a year or more of research and development, and challenged the workers involved, as well as the audience, to think differently about their labor. How did an artist from New York engender the space and freedom to do this from within such distinct bureaucratic municipal systems? You could say that Ukeles has a distinct ability to seamlessly move in and out of different parts of civic operations and make links where none existed before, all the while posing questions that turned views on labor upside down. In conjunction with this, she invited workers—as well as organizational leaders in New York and children in Givors—to cocreate a new work ballet each time, opening up spaces of artistic possibility through choreographic imagination.

Concerned with some of the most pressing issues of contemporaneity—urbanism, ecology, and feminism—over the past four decades Ukeles has pioneered how we perceive and ultimately engage in maintenance activities. The work ballets derive from Ukeles's engagement in the sanitation operations of New York City in order to comprehend how city infrastructures work though grand-scale coordination and cooperation. Ukeles began to question the operations of maintenance in the late 1960s after giving birth to her first child, and afterward being consumed by the labor required to sustain everyday life. She found her life divided: half of the week she devoted to motherhood and the other half to her art practice. The invisible and underappreciated work that makes up much of daily life, the hidden maintenance often done by women—cooking, cleaning, caretaking—led Ukeles to write the groundbreaking "Manifesto for Maintenance Art, 1969!" in which she communicated her ideas regarding maintenance, beginning from personal experiences, and expanding to society and the earth as a whole. In the manifesto, still a cornerstone of her work today, she affirms that as an artist, everything she does is art. As a means of grasping and making sense of her own condition and to define it as a framework for making art, she wrote:

Everything I say is Art is Art. Everything I do is Art is Art. "We have no Art, we try to do everything well." (Balinese saying).

Avant-garde art, which claims utter development, is infected by strains of maintenance ideas, maintenance activities, and maintenance materials.

Conceptual & Process art, especially, claim pure development and change, yet employ almost purely maintenance processes.

This early thinking around work and labor is central to her later ballets, where the injection of art into maintenance systems begets "maintenance art" out of mundane operations, making room in an otherwise rigid system for creativity, new modes of collaboration, and, by and large, play. No one knows what play will end up like; making the play is always exciting and unpredictable for the players and the audience. It is the participation of the drivers in Ukeles's work ballets and understanding their performance as a playful synthesis of work and art, in all its uncertainties, that makes it meaningful. According to philosopher Hans-Georg Gadamer: "Play fulfills its purpose only if the player loses himself in play. Seriousness is not merely something that calls us away from play; rather seriousness in playing is necessary to make the play wholly play."[1]

At the Wadsworth Atheneum Museum of Art, Hartford, in 1973, as a maintenance artwork and her first public performance, Ukeles literally cleaned the museum for eight hours straight, outside and inside. She mopped the floors and washed the front steps of the museum, making this often hidden but necessary work visible in public space and in broad daylight during opening hours, in contrast to the usual cleaning of the museum that happened when it was closed. This series of four performances manifested the enormous exertion needed to keep the museum a pristine white cube, and can also be seen as an early example of institutional critique, which brought about a critical reevaluation of the inner organizational workings of art institutions and the sociopolitical and economic con-

text that surrounds them, while taking our attention to the very spatial characteristics of the museum.

Perhaps Ukeles's most widely known work is *Touch Sanitation* (1977–80), a multifaceted, multiyear project. One component was *Handshake Ritual* (1979): over the course of eleven months she traveled to every single New York City sanitation garage, transfer station, incinerator, repair shop, and landfill to personally shake the hands of the entire department's sanitation men. This was a massive undertaking to say the least, which involved coordination from every facet of the department and a mapping of all five boroughs, which changed repeatedly due to the weather and the establishment of new community-board requirements. Ukeles met all 8,500 workers and thanked them one by one for "keeping New York City alive." This gesture symbolically—and for some, actually—restored the dignity of labor to the workforce of an entire city agency that was often neglected and reproached for their work, for the reason alone that they dealt with the refuse of society. During *Touch Sanitation* Ukeles's day began at roll call in each sanitation garage, 6:00 a.m. in the summer and 7:00 a.m. in the winter, where she explained how she would make a sculpture of "the whole city's underbelly." As *Touch Sanitation* progressed, she would periodically copy the sanitation workers' actions for the day as part of the performance, mirroring all their movements, their daily work choreography. This component, titled *Follow in Your Footsteps* (1979–80), came out of Ukeles's determination to develop credibility with the sanitation workers, experience their level of exposure, and learn their skill sets. She joined the sanitation men for their "public performance" on the street where a mostly silent "audience" peered at them from behind blinds or curtains in their homes. Copying the workers' movements for efficiency as they lifted and emptied garbage cans into their trucks, Ukeles learned the delicate and great balance needed for the heavy lifting, which she likened to a dance. A kind of "dancing in the street" for Ukeles, this performance led her to "understand how to keep something in motion" and also made the workers laugh during their endless lifting of steel garbage cans.[2] Constantly responding to what was happening on the street, and within the department, *Touch Sanitation*, like the work ballets, was an ever-shifting endeavor, bending to the participants and city itself.

The abovementioned works underscore the way in which Ukeles embeds herself in a system of operations for her practice to unfold. While communication,

Touch Sanitation: Follow in Your Footsteps, 1977–80. Citywide performance with 8,500 New York City sanitation workers.

coordination, and a "love for people in the space of labor" is inherent in all her work, for most projects she reinvents her methods based on the specific framework of each system she engages. What defines these works as well as much of Ukeles's practice is that she operates decidedly from within, engaging with the operations of a place on every level, whether it's New York or Rotterdam, from the drivers of the vehicles and barges to their bosses and city officials. Ukeles introduces art into mechanical work and proposes alternative ways to approach skilled but repetitive labor, and at the same time she makes the value of this work evident. Each work ballet shared the same underlying proposition: to cocreate choreographed performances with drivers based on their highly expert knowledge of vehicles and barges, effecting new imaginative ways for them to participate in their work through collective action and civil engagement.

To digress for a moment, my first introduction to Ukeles's work occurred fifteen years ago, when I assisted with the production of *Penetration and Transparency: Morphed* (2001–02), her contribution

to a group exhibition on the closure of the Fresh Kills landfill on Staten Island. Ukeles's newly commissioned work was a six-channel video installation that documented those she named "pathfinders"—ecologists, sanitation officials, landscape architects, and cultural thinkers, among others—on walks through the about-to-close Fresh Kills (now the site of a future park and Ukeles's long-term NYC Percent for Art commission, slated to open in 2016). In the videos, the experts gave their individual perspectives and visions for what she called the "fifty-year social sculpture made by each of us," a manmade expanse of the remnants of society.[3]

Ukeles's work delves into many collective sociopolitical ideas and histories; however, it always starts from the individual's relationship to support structures, those that preserve and sustain life. Having grown up

1   Hans-Georg Gadamer, *Truth and Method* (New York: Seabury Press, 1975), 107.
2   Unless otherwise noted, all quotes are from Mierle Laderman Ukeles during conversations with the author in fall 2014.
3   See Olivia Georgia and Kari Conte, eds., *Fresh Kills: Artists Respond to the Closure of the Staten Island Landfill, October 14, 2001–May 27, 2002* (Staten Island, NY: Snug Harbor Cultural Center, 2002).

in an outer borough of New York City, which in many ways was considered a backstage to Manhattan, this has been particularly clear to me. That periphery, inevitably, was home to many city workers, providing me with an up-close view of the substrate of labor that keeps the city going, and the negligible value assigned to such work. Ukeles's practice has shown that art can collapse boundaries and meaningfully enter everyday life, to enact change on multiple levels. From this position, Ukeles makes art from life, and her own active and genuine way of being-in-the-world is what gives it agency.

During my research for the Fresh Kills exhibition catalogue I was surprised to find that no monograph had been written on Ukeles's significant contributions. More than a decade later this is still the case for many pivotal artists of her generation who privileged situation making over object making. *Mierle Laderman Ukeles: Seven Work Ballets* is the first monograph on Ukeles's practice, and is as much an artist's book as an art-historical publication on the work ballets. The outcome of five years of conversations between Mierle, myself, and many others, the book revisits the work ballets through firsthand accounts and extensive archival research. Nearly all of the 125 photographs and drawings documenting the work ballets in the following chapters are accessible for the first time through this book.

That Ukeles was able to recall twenty or thirty years later such precise details of what transpired in the work ballets is owed largely to her methodical archival practice. At her office inside the New York City Department of Sanitation—where she has been the official, unsalaried Artist-in-Residence for the past thirty-eight years—a monumental archive exists, over one thousand feet long, that includes correspondence, articles, choreographic drawings, and daily notes for each work ballet. This treasure trove reveals that for Ukeles, the actual work on each project begins the moment she writes her first letter for support, and not when the performance itself begins. At the same time, this archive contributes to the historiography of the city agencies that she collaborated with, especially those in New York City.

Performative and collaborative art is difficult to grasp solely through visual documentation, and so the stories of what happened in the work ballets—so vividly written here by Ukeles—are paramount and offer the reader the opportunity to be a second audience, experiencing the work through firsthand accounts. In that regard, the importance of writing in Ukeles's

practice cannot be underestimated. Her conviction is so tangible even in her daily correspondence with city agencies. She has literally pried open these bureaucratic systems for art.

There has been much written in recent years on socially engaged and participatory art. However, Ukeles's approach is distinct from much of this writing. The anxieties, hopes, and challenges faced by artists who make this work are often hidden from the public. The chapters that follow, on each of the seven work ballets, make apparent the high degree of risk in collaborative art making that is often invisible to the public. Ukeles relinquishes creative control in order to co-imagine with others in municipal agencies where there is usually no precedent for play and creativity within the sphere of the workday. But most of all, Ukeles's writing amplifies how, in collaborative projects, communication and social relations are the most important instruments for the work, and problem solving, social interaction, negotiation, persuasion, and coordination are the work's material, just as much as the end performance and documentation.

Each ballet was a response to a new commission, and Ukeles embarked on rigorous fieldwork by gathering local knowledge in each city. Fieldwork, a term that originated in cultural anthropology, can increasingly be applied to the way artists work. Conceptual art practices of the 1960s interwove research and production. Artistic fieldwork takes location and mobility as its tools, and produces new knowledge through a convergence of diverse disciplines, systematic research, and, more importantly, intuition. In this sense, the work ballets provide a more locational read-

Fernand Léger, *Ballet Mécanique*, 1924. Film still. Courtesy of Anthology Film Archives.

ing of their contexts through the embodied knowledge that Ukeles gained from all the various participants: from the tugboat captain in *Marrying the Barges: A Barge Ballet*, to the members of the Steelworkers Organization of Active Retirees in Pittsburgh, to the children of Givors. Yvonne Rainer's task- and game-like choreography from the 1960s is also relevant to the work ballets. In particular, Rainer's approach to combining task-based movements and language within her dances was influential to Ukeles.

The first work ballet, *Sanitation Celebrations*, was part of New York City's inaugural art parade in 1983. It was conceived of as a "love letter to the city,"[4] and New York, at the time in financial ruin, was deeply in need of such goodwill. *Sanitation Celebrations* was a three-movement procession. The first was *The Social Mirror*, an actual garbage truck covered in mirrors, which reflected the viewers, bringing them face-to-face with themselves as active makers of waste in an advanced capitalist society. *Ceremonial Sweep*, the third and final movement, put sanitation in the parade, as opposed to its usual place outside of it; here, administrators and political leaders took the brooms from sanitation men and swept the detritus left over from the parade. Between these two movements was *Ballet Mécanique for Six Mechanical Sweepers*, a ballet choreographed over several days with the drivers of mechanical street sweepers; six street sweepers performed masterful rhythmic moves in relation to each other and suggestive of, alternately, a snake, a spider, and a figure 8.

Fernand Léger's 1924 avant-garde film *Ballet Mécanique* was a precedent for Ukeles's mechanical-sweepers ballet. Its nonnarrative, pulsating black-and-white footage cuts between man and machine, illustrating the increasing synthesis of both in the industrial age, and the influences of Dada, Cubist, and Futurist ideas about the mechanical age. Repetitions are critical to the film, as in dance: swinging pistons, gears, and parts usher in a new era of technological uncertainty set to a score of sirens, airplane propellers, bells, and pianos.

While aspects of Ukeles's work ballets are grounded in the avant-garde legacies of Futurism and Constructivism, their vision and intent differ, and they grow out of a commitment to democracy, a "democratic culture which is built on the ineffable value of each individual human being." Also integral to the historical lineage of the work ballets are the rapid developments in dance as a medium that took place at the same time as the evolution of machine culture at the beginning

Karl Grill, Spiral Costume, from the *Triadic Ballet* by Oskar Schlemmer, 1926. Gelatin silver print, 22.5 × 16.2 cm. Courtesy of the J. Paul Getty Museum, Los Angeles.

of the twentieth century. This simultaneity led many Futurists to consider mechanization, speed, and dynamism through the lens of choreography and dance. Italian poet and founder of the Futurist movement F. T. Marinetti organized many "Futurist evenings" that served as political and performative gatherings where the numerous manifestos of Futurism were read. He also wrote the "Manifesto of Futurist Dance" (1917), in which he outlined the first three Futurist dances derived from the chief mechanisms of war: shrapnel, the machine gun, and the airplane. In it, he writes, "One must imitate the movements of machines with gestures; pay assiduous court to steering wheels, ordinary wheels, pistons, thereby preparing the fusion of man with the machine, to achieve the metallicity of the Futurist dance."[5] Intrinsically kinetic, dance was a logi-

4   Creative Time, announcement for the First New York City Art Parade.
5   Quoted in Felicia M. McCarren, *Dancing Machines: Choreographies of the Age of Mechanical Reproduction* (Stanford, CA: Stanford University Press, 2003), 104.

cal form for the Futurists to present their ideas about technology, motion, and progress.

Machine aesthetics also commanded Giacomo Balla's *Fireworks* from 1917, a "light ballet" that was accompanied by a Stravinsky score. Eliminating performers and instead enacting modernity with stage lights on moving geometric sets, it curiously formed a part of the Ballets Russes program. Also fusing the machine and ballet was the Bauhaus artist Oskar Schlemmer's *Triadic Ballet* (1922), a dance made up of multiples of three in regard to dancers and acts, and based on choreography that the artist called "ground geometry." The ballet's intricate and heavily restrictive costumes were made from aluminum foil, fiberglass rods, glass, wire, celluloid, and other metallic materials. Limiting the dancer's movements, these unwieldy costumes determined and inspired the ballet's choreography. In a sense, the dancer's body was removed from the ballet, and instead the dancers became the "conductors" of the costume-apparatus, enacting scenes that ranged from humorous to serious.

Ukeles's fourth work ballet, *Movin' On Along: Barge and Towboat Ballet* (1992), took place in the steel and glass manufacturing city of Pittsburgh, where the Allegheny, Monongahela, and Ohio Rivers meet. Initially, Ukeles had wanted to coordinate the movement of trains above the rivers on bridges with more trains below alongside boats and barges. Proving too difficult to organize in the short time frame allotted before the performance, Ukeles started working instead on a ballet that showed that great industry still exists in Pittsburgh, particularly on the rivers, with steel, aluminum, and glass from the "flow of recycling."

Working across city agencies, and innovating the means and structures for a new collaboration between them, for the first movement Ukeles had the rivers cleared for a ballet with three barges filled with recyclables. Similar to *Marrying the Barges*—Ukeles's second work ballet that took place in New York City in 1984—*Movin' On Along* allowed the captains and crew of the barges and push boats the opportunity to try maneuvers they rarely attempted, and for an audience.

The second movement involved the Steelworkers Organization of Active Retirees, a group that worked to have healthcare restored to those who were abandoned by the bankrupt steel companies where they'd formerly worked. Ukeles had invited them to participate in the ballet. Learning of the hand gestures they had used to communicate with each other on the noisy factory floor, she choreographed a demon-

Arseny Avraamov conducting the last *Symphony of Sirens* using two flaming torches, Moscow, c. 1923. Image from René Fülöp-Miller, *Geist und Gesicht des Bolschewismus: Darstellung und Kritik des kulturellen Lebens in Sowjet-Russland* (Zurich: Amalthea-Verlag, 1926).

stration based on these gestures, with their demands on placards.

Seventy years earlier in 1922, from the pinnacle of a tower in Baku, the Azerbaijani capital, the composer Arseny Avraamov conducted the utterly monumental, citywide *Symphony of Sirens*, an event that links to the work ballets. Avraamov, a founder of Proletkult, was deeply engaged with the technological future of music. A public sound event that overtook the port, the symphony had an entire Caspian flotilla at its helm, and the performance entailed a successive series of sounds exclusive to machines and factories and "played" by infantry, locomotives, factory sirens, machine guns, airplanes, and canons. Each contributor to the symphony was signaled to begin and stop by a different colored flag waved by Avraamov. In tandem, choirs performed an industrial workers' anthem and steam whistles that Avraamov invented especially for the occasion.

Avraamov believed that every city has its own symphony, and he required the participation of many to realize it. This was the third and most ambitious iteration of the symphony, with previous versions taking place in different Russian cities from 1919 to 1923. Avraamov wrote a detailed score with instructions so that it could be played by anyone in the future; remarkably, the symphony was reconstructed in 2003 in Russia with a precise musical arrangement that was spatially organized to reproduce its original acoustic depth. In the same sense—as discussed by Shannon Jackson and Tom Finkelpearl in the conversation at the end of this book—Ukeles's ballet works, especially with such careful chronicles of their choreography and movements in this book, have the potential to be performed again in the future.

Ukeles's work ballets utilize technology and industry in the aim of meaningful change. In this way, her practice intentionally materializes the Russian avant-garde legacies of the Constructivists, who practically developed their ideas, and the later Productivists, who philosophically dealt with the merging of art and industry. Both movements were influenced by the Futurists and aspired to bring the dynamism of the modern era into art that participated in industry with new useful ways to work.

Much like Ukeles later on, the Constructivists made art for the benefit of society, with the spectator becoming an active participant in the social project. They wanted to move art out of the studio and theater into everyday life, in order to work with *real* space and materials. Futurist Vladimir Mayakovski wrote in his poem "Order to the Army of Art" (1918) that artists should work in public space, where "the streets are our brushes; the squares are our palettes." Echoing these same concerns, for *Touch Sanitation Performance* (1977–80) Ukeles asked sanitation workers where the "exhibition" should be located. Their answers led her to locate part of *Touch Sanitation Show* (1980–84) in an actual sanitation facility with trucks and barges, in addition to the Ronald Feldman Gallery in SoHo. Ukeles wrote in her announcement for the exhibition, "One of the best things a worker said was, 'Look. You're not a normal artist. You're a REAL artist. This show has to be real with trucks and barges. So why can't they see what it's like here?'"

In particular, the work ballets are connected to Constructivism's theater and mass performances. Often incorporating actors who performed mechani-cal gestures, Constructivist theater built stage sets to mimic machines, with rotating scaffolds, platforms, and wheels. These sets served as ideal platforms for biomechanics, which trained actors to perform rhythmic movements originally designed for worker efficiency. The founder of biomechanics, Vsevolod Meyerhold, also proposed a theater where the audience sat level to a stage that was open to the street, debunking its artificial nature.

In 1920, on the third anniversary of the Russian Revolution, Nikolai Evreinov organized the mass re-enactment *The Storming of the Winter Palace* with the participation of eight thousand performers. Two platforms were constructed in front of the palace. A red one was for the Red Army and those that took part in the original event, and a white one for the provisional government with ballet dancers and circus artists, among others. A symphony was played and workers stormed the palace, followed by fireworks and an army parade.

Ukeles's work ballets rely on collaboration with already existing networks to cocreate her work. The fusion of workers' existing skill sets and Ukeles's artistic élan led to different ways of thinking and approaching their labor. The strict requirements and rigorous systems imposed on government work leave little room for experimentation and abstract thinking. Created in close collaboration with the drivers, the ballets have an inherent productive dichotomy: cultural labor is presented as a way to initiate conversation about the very conditions and context of actual manual labor.

In fact, it was crucial for all the rehearsals and performances of the work ballets to occur within the drivers' regular workday. The ballets suggest that through repetition of work, bodily gestures are codified, managed, and governed. By initiating a nonproductive artistic activity into this sphere, Ukeles dissolves the polarity between intellectual and manual labor. Manual labor, in fact, requires skill sets that take years to master, contrary to widespread ideas about the simplicity of learning such labor.

Each of Ukeles's performances is truly collaborative and makes possible what otherwise wouldn't be through the creative contributions of workers. In other words, the work ballets are imagined, created, and choreographed together with the workers through an extensive being-together and dialogue, showing "the worker as culture-maker" and highlighting the significant talent and skill of each. As a project that is dependent on a specific site, municipal system, and culture, each ballet required Ukeles to reinvent her process and building blocks, learning new skills and putting aside others.

In Givors, the site of Ukeles's fifth work ballet, *Re-spect for Givors* (1993), the division between performers and audience was even less than in previous ballets—the city in its entirety was a stage on which the choreography unfolded. Similarly, in its use of the city as stage, Daniel Buren's *Seven Ballets in Manhattan* (1975) instructed five dancers to walk as if in protest on a preplanned route for two hours each day, holding up placards of Buren's minimal and abstract stripe paintings.

A highway was built in the 1980s that cut right through the French town of Givors, leading to a general deterioration of living standards for its population of 19,000. Like with *Touch Sanitation*, the situation inspired Ukeles to deal with the city as a whole, linking land and water to thread the different constituents together. The town was looking to regenerate urban space. Many children from immigrant families who lived in public housing, for example, had never been to the center of the city. Although their families had been living there for two generations, they were still called *les étrangers*. Giving respect back to themselves, and restoring their dignity of labor, the workers from the sanitation, parks, and fire departments collaborated with Ukeles to choreograph a two-part ballet: first on the main road and then a three-movement ballet that went along the river. It began with a parade in the center of town with all twenty-seven municipal vehicles and children from the housing estates at the city's outskirts. The children created and wore their own special costumes. All the city workers were dismissed for the day of the performance to gather and watch the ballet. The participation of the city workers in Givors, both as viewers and drivers, collapsed the conventional barriers between the audience and performance, effecting a "revolution during office hours."[6] Through the ballets, the workers actively participated in rethinking the creative potential of their work, bringing them closer to their own labor.

A ballet requires boundless creative intelligence and skill, and the dancer's body must operate like a machine. It has often been said that the real work of the dancer is to make the difficult look effortless; Ukeles's work ballets unveil the complex training needed to master the work of the drivers. Equally important is the ballet's intention to burst open the space for imagination and joy within the routinization of work. The work ballets resonate with the central ideas of the last two centuries. Labor, technology, and organization permeated all aspects of life in the twentieth century; the key concept of the twenty-first century so far is connection. Now, whenever I see a street sweeper or garbage truck in New York City, the deft movements of the drivers and vehicles appear as choreography for a dance unfolding on the city streets for us all.

6   Mierle Laderman Ukeles, lecture at Marabouparken, Stockholm, March 24, 2015.

ARTIST'S INTRODUCTION

Dear Reader,

This is a story of seven public projects—work ballets—by an artist crazy about the public domain as our common home, wild about public systems, infrastructure, and public workers. I tried to provoke the limits of severely restricted work systems, to pry all this open a bit, to spring service workers out of frozen clichés, to sing out that they are all part of creating a culture that is alive.

This is also a story of efforts made by regions, cities, and municipal agencies to see themselves anew. In six of the seven commissions, I was invited to create an artwork (which turned into a work ballet) due to attempts by public bodies to rethink and perhaps reinvent systems and even whole areas.[1] These were places that had become overlooked, dismissed, denigrated, and depopulated. An idea emerged that artists might have something to offer in a troubled public environment. That notion made these works possible.

These seven work ballets show the relationship between culture and maintenance. I believe that one measure of a democratic culture's greatness is how it envisions service work and how service workers are valued. It is these workers upon whom we are utterly dependent to be able to live in a city—they enable the removal of garbage and recyclables, snow, the cleaning of streets—so that in our everyday existence we can act in a clear present, and we don't have to be slogging through and swamped by what happened yesterday. An unwillingness to acknowledge this dependency is literally infantile—the new infant thinks she is all-powerful, an autonomous world. But on the other hand, the service worker is dependent upon the public to make a living and be provided with the budget, equipment, materials, and supplies to enable him/her to work safely and with quality.

I'm always asking: What is the relationship between dependency and power and dependency and value? So it's not just dependency on the one hand and power on the other that I have aimed to reveal in these works. It is beyond all that. With this book, and in these works, I have been drawing an invitation to move to a social state of interdependence.

Art must be about freedom and free choice. I always say this to the workers when I invite them to create these works with me, and that each person can certainly refuse to participate. It is vital to me that people's participation is voluntary. This is to create a contrast between the work they accept they have to do, no matter how they feel that day, and the artwork. It has to be different.

I purposely pick zones of activity that are utterly necessary but also highly constrained. I also always pick groups where the workers were already highly skilled even though a strict line of authority was present. Their skill didn't rule; the boss ruled. That was the deal they had already accepted in order to work and be paid. Art aims to burst through all of this, to illuminate the individual who possesses a boundless spirit beyond all rules. If I could create something that piggybacked on their skill and knowledge, thus tapping into the power inherent in trafficking in necessity, and yet offer a space of freedom and free choice, I felt we could create something new.

These artworks reveal the workers who operate the very machines of real life, in the streets, squares, and waterways, doing extraordinary things—full of flairs of freedom, of fantasy, of free choice, yet full of the skills that denote great power. Skill joined with freedom and fantasy yields the idea of a new kind of power for the viewer as well as the participant. This creates a lens through which one can see an individual artist and an individual worker acting freely—in the midst of a system of constraint.

Because the artwork lies so close to what we accept as reality, it constantly interrogates and even shakes the notion of necessity. Is it necessary to work like this? Must we accept this whole net of constraints? In their wake, these artworks open up the possibility of reinventing our relationship to reality itself.[2]

METHOD

In these work ballets, when the focus was narrowed down to a few days of rehearsal and a definite end performance date, I brought with me a commitment to not tell people what to do. I invited them in but I was not the boss. Obviously, my work had gone through many levels of approval from authorities, or I wouldn't have been able to enter a room, a hall, a boat, with a certain number of workers released from their regular work for a certain amount of days. But once we were in the room together, my theory of inviting them to participate and not telling them what to do had its space and power. The space, the power, and the authority I handed over to share with the workers yielded a tremendous response from them in each ballet. I had a trust in them. I really did admire their skills and felt that the general public did not see their skill level or them as powerful individuals. I had to enter a vacuum when I first met each group. I refused to be the authority for them. I needed enough time for them to begin to believe that I meant it, even while not knowing what would happen, even though I had so much at stake, and for them to take their own chances and assert themselves into the artwork. It was extremely risky and extremely scary for me personally.

Something rose up between us and among us. Out of this vacuum. It didn't exist before. What rose up and coalesced was the art and the resulting artwork. Not one of us made or could make these works individually. We created it among ourselves.

How did I know how to do this? Essentially by trusting myself as an artist. This method was made up in the same way that I had always made my art: going into the blank place of not knowing—where you don't know what you're doing—and inventing my way out of there. My art comes from that point in my gut. But now working with others, I knew that I had to hand over sole authority. *Let it rise up among us. Don't tell them what to do. Take extreme risks. That is the essence.* My deep respect for their skills and trust in their creativity came through without giving up on my trust in myself as a creator. It opened a huge space of invention and energy every single time!

WHAT IS THE ARTWORK?

Besides the ballet themselves, the chapters contain descriptions of the process. This isn't a choreography book, but a book about the growth of the artworks between the artist and workers. I consider the process a part of the art—the invention of the site, the development of both the "characters" in the ballet and what constitutes the ballet, including the creation of organizational processes to form material structures used in the pieces, and working with people on the job who don't normally work with artists. I think, looking back, that I was trying to create a shift in reality itself about what constitutes work and how artists collaborating with workers can stretch the limits of work.

I regard the whole process of making these work ballets as the artwork because invention and creation operated throughout. The basic infrastructure for these works didn't exist before. Thus the artwork, in my view, includes the research, the original proposals, the negotiations with authorities about what aspects of the proposals could happen, the meetings, connecting with the workers, and the process of making with them, our rehearsals, the unexpected things. And also, of course, the performances themselves.

New York City, June 2015

1   This was the case with my ballets in New York City (as the city emerged from the dire fiscal crisis of the 1970s and early 1980s), Pittsburgh, Givors, and Echigo-Tsumari. Only Rotterdam was different, since it was apparent that their public service workers and systems were so highly appreciated.
2   In some projects, you will see gaps between my proposal and its realization in the performance. Some components of proposals were not accepted (sometimes the insanely ambitious elements). This was often due to what curators and authorities never tired of reminding me—the constraints of my very unusual and mostly in-kind budgets that translated into limitations of scale, numbers of participants and vehicles, duration of in-person interaction with workers, and days of rehearsals, all of which needed to happen during regular (costly) working hours. I am leaving in what didn't happen, because I think the visions in the proposals have artistic validity in themselves. As well, other artists can see what could have happened, can see what did happen, and expand zones of what will happen in the future.

I.

SANITATION CELEBRATIONS

THE GRAND FINALE
OF THE FIRST NEW YORK CITY
ART PARADE

INTRODUCTION TO
SANITATION CELEBRATIONS

Late in 1976, I was invited to visit the New York City Department of Sanitation (DSNY) to explore making maintenance art with them. At that time, I had been making art about maintenance systems and with maintenance workers for about eight years. I was thrilled at this opportunity because "NYC Sanitation" was the major league of the whole maintenance world. I then spent a year and a half doing research, during which I made a series of mega-proposals called "Maintenance Art Works Meets the Department of Sanitation: Projects." One of these was called "Work/Art Festival: San Truck Rodeo & Sanman Skills Competition: Festival on City Streets."

I wanted to create a situation that would make the skills of these workers visible as cultural actions—to pop them out of a near universal feeling among sanitation workers where they did their work in public but, strangely, the public didn't seem to see them, certainly not as persons with highly developed skills. I had always wanted to do something to rupture that perception.

In 1977, I went to the New York City St. Patrick's Day Parade, one of the major annual parades in the city, to research how sanitation is presented in the parade. I did see some of their officers marching along with other uniformed services, like police and fire; nothing unusual. But then I saw something else. Behind the horses on parade, I saw several sanita-

tion workers in quite shabby uniforms (common during the fiscal crisis of the 1970s), bent over, sweeping the horses' droppings to the side. It was their posture that gripped me. I couldn't get the image of them bent over out of my mind, and it led me to develop a whole theory of parades. What is a parade? In a city, there is usually a taboo against staring at people on the street. You can stare at someone for a certain limited amount of time, and then if you continue staring, it definitely turns things weird. Everyone knows this unspoken rule; no one has to teach it to you. It's a kind of primitive city rite that just gets passed along. In a parade, on the other hand, this taboo against staring is dropped. You can stare as long as you want, wantonly. The other half of this deal, however, is that the people on parade usually present themselves in very formal ways, almost armored, to protect themselves against this permission to stare at them. Their movements are scripted. They stand up very straight. They are "on parade." This posture is opposite that of the working sanitation workers, who were not armored, nor were they displaying themselves; they were working. They were trapped into being watched. It was hard to be sweeping up horse droppings while everyone was watching you. I noticed that when they swept the droppings over to the side, where the members of the public were behind police barricades, some workers often did the last shove of the broom, pushing the droppings "out of the way of the parade route" with a little extra gusto—nearer and nearer to the parade viewers. I saw people turning away from the parade to look down at their shoes, nervous that the droppings were coming their way.

And then, there were the workers in mechanical sweepers at the end of the parade, facing mountains of trampled confetti and grungy debris, waiting to do the picky and demanding work of erasing the celebration and returning the streets back to everyday reality. They also were not part of the excitement, on parade. They were *after* the end.

I promised myself, right there in 1977, that one day I would create a work where regular sanitation workers were *in* the parade, *of* the parade, *were* the parade, proudly on show, even as the grand finale, not what comes after.

INVITATION TO PARTICIPATE IN THE FIRST NEW YORK CITY ART PARADE AND MY PROPOSAL

I got my chance in 1983, when Anita Contini, co-founder and director of Creative Time, Martha Wilson, founder and director of Franklin Furnace Archive, and Ed Jones, curator at the New Museum of Contemporary Art, nominated me for the grand finale of the First New York City Art Parade. I was raring to go.

After presenting my ideas to the art parade organizers who represented over 100 arts organizations participating in the parade, I got a letter from the project director Henry Korn, saying, "Hey Garbage! . . . You can absolutely count on taking charge of the grand finale of the Art Parade!" It was to be part of the annual Museum Mile festival inaugurating the art season, and would run thirty-two blocks south on Madison Avenue. Since Madison Avenue runs north, this switch would require completely closing this major street.

There was a lot of passion at the time for this Art Parade, which was seen as a mark that the city was coming alive again and climbing out of the pit of the severe fiscal crisis of the 1970s and early 1980s, where the city almost had to declare bankruptcy and 20 percent of its workforce had been cut. There was an appetite to do something unique in support of the artists of New York City.

I proposed a grand finale for the parade involving DSNY, sanitation workers, and significant others. It would be a three-movement work ballet: the first would be *The Social Mirror*, the second would be *Ballet Mécanique for Six Mechanical Sweepers*, and the third would be *Ceremonial Sweep*.

After many rounds of negotiation, Sanitation Commissioner Norman Steisel accepted my proposal on April 27, 1983. Critically, he sent his approval memo the same day to First Deputy Commissioner Vincent Whitfield and to Deputy Commissioner of Public Affairs Vito Turso, directing them to provide operations and media support throughout the agency. This was a breakthrough, since I myself had no staff. In August, Henry Korn wrote to Commissioner Steisel: "Under your leadership the Department of Sanitation has become a powerful cultural force."

PREPARATION OF MOVEMENT I: THE SOCIAL MIRROR[1]

The concept was natural, obvious: a garbage truck covered in mirrors so that its familiar moving shape—every two-year-old kid already recognized it—would now reflect the city street and those in the street back at themselves, capturing them within the frame. This could "prove" that those who were dependent on sanitation and the sanitation workers were always in a two-way relationship: It's-my-garbage-not-their-garbage. The environment would literally adhere to *The Social Mirror*, and interdependence would be caught within its reflectivity. I wanted to show that sanitation was the beginning, not outside, of urban culture, that sanitation makes the city possible.

With the go-ahead from Commissioner Steisel, and an anonymous donation for expenses from "a friend who loves New York City,"[2] a twenty-cubic-yard "M Series" garbage collection truck appeared, having been "borrowed by headquarters" from a perplexed superintendent (who never got it back—I'm told he was steaming!). We brought it in for a "fitting" to the main fabricating floor of Colonial Mirror in Brooklyn. Twenty-three feet ten inches long from the front of the cab to the tip of the hopper,[3] seven feet wide, and five feet ten inches high, it was like bringing a bull into a china shop. The garbage truck, positioned among many fragile mirrored objects, stood patiently and was thoroughly measured for tempered glass mirrors to cover the large flat planes of the sides, flexible acrylic mirrors for the great curves of the hopper, and smoky acrylic mirrors for the structural ribs. To my regret, the cab would not be mirrored—too expensive. After the custom-sized glass mirrors were cut and hand tempered, the truck was moved to another smaller glass company in Brooklyn, where several fabricators went to work transforming the truck into the artwork under my direction. This unique vehicle was given a new Department of Sanitation designation—25M-271 A. F. F. (Auxiliary Field Force)—on September 17, 1983.

PREPARATION OF MOVEMENT II: BALLET MÉCANIQUE FOR SIX MECHANICAL SWEEPERS

I asked for the best mechanical broom drivers to work with me. Mechanical sweeper vehicles, or mechanical brooms as they were called, were very different from garbage trucks as they only cleaned the streets. The rotating circular curb brooms of these unique vehicles worked primarily in the junction where the street met the curb, wetting down and dislodging stuck debris, then sucked them up into the hopper. The big roller broom in front got the rest. New York City was measurably dirtier in those days than now.

I had ridden in sweepers several times since 1977, while researching the DSNY. We rode very high up; it was very bouncy and incredibly noisy. What I saw with my own eyes when I was inside the vehicle was how crazy the New York City streets were. Despite there being signs posted on all the streets prohibiting parking at scheduled times so the sweepers could get to the curb, people flagrantly ignored these regulations and parked cars right up to the curb when it was supposed to be cleared for cleaning. Not only was there one lane of cars, but also often two lanes of cars, and even triple-parked cars. What was the driver supposed to do? He would wiggle in as close as possible, but then he would have to go around these cars and leave that spot or spots unclean. Then everyone got mad at the drivers that the streets were so dirty. On an everyday basis, it was incredibly frustrating. They generally made the best of what they could do, leaving a trail of arcs as they had to circumvent illegally parked cars.

So I promised myself that one day, I would clear away the traffic, the double- and triple-parked cars, and let people see just how talented, coolheaded, and inventive these drivers were. This would be the second movement. I thought of it immediately as a new *ballet mécanique*, growing out of traditions in Russian Constructivist art, Futurism, Cubist films, and the film of Fernand Léger.

This would be the first work ballet that I created with drivers and their special vehicles. The negotiations for how many drivers and vehicles were very intense and went on for months, because it was very expensive to take these workers off the job for rehearsals and then the ballet. "How many mechanical brooms do you want?" they asked. I asked for six, so there could be different kinds of combinations besides a single line such as three couples of two vehicles working together or two clusters of three vehicles. Accepted. I got one day for a first meeting with the drivers and three days after that over the next week for rehearsals with the final rehearsal the week before the parade. A simulation of the long parade route was set up at the DSNY driver-training facilities on Randall's Island in the East River for the rehearsals. The lanes in this huge open space were marked according to the dimensions of Madison Avenue: fifty-four feet wide curb to curb and many city blocks long. We were told not to plan moves wider than thirty-six to forty feet wide by two hundred feet long. Since I had never done anything like this before, I tried to ask for more time, but it was too expensive. I was lucky to get what I got.

I arrived on the first day and met the six drivers. They were drawn from all over the city, did not know each other, and had not worked with each other before. I had heard that they were fantastic drivers and that they are so devoted to their jobs that they "simonize their sweepers."[4] They looked pretty nervous, as if asking themselves, what am I doing here? We went into a small one-room building on the edge of the field. I explained how much time we had to plan this ballet—three days starting tomorrow—and that the ballet would end up running thirty-two blocks down Madison Avenue as the grand finale of the First New York City Art Parade. We sat down and looked at each other. I was so scared!

They said, "Tell us what you want us to do." I gulped and said, "No. That's not the way this will work. I have not made any plans in advance. I'm an artist. I'm not your supervisor. I have some ideas, but you are the experts of your vehicles. Not me. I really admire so much what you do; I want to show this to the audience. I hope that we can create something together. I invite you to come up with movements that we can do, to create this ballet together. There has to

1   I had first proposed this public sculpture to DSNY on February 5, 1979, calling it *See Sanitation—See Yourself* (the proposal is presented in full on page 31). It was accepted conceptually by DSNY in 1979, but it took four years to fund and find a venue to show it.
2   I met the donor only once in June 1983. He said he wished to remain anonymous, then told me why he was doing this: "Let's not hold back the dawn. It will be a showstopper!"
3   The hopper sometimes refers to the entire hollow body of the truck—the largest component that contains the garbage. In New York City, the hopper also can refer to the huge packer blade that forms the curving end of the body and is used to compress the garbage in order to make more space inside. This also becomes the first area into which the garbage is dumped. Packer blades are controlled through a hydraulic system operated by the worker, and are capable of exerting large pressure to compress the waste.
4   Simoniz is a special car wax that yields a super hard shine to the vehicle, usually a hot rod.

be an aspect of free expression for it to be art. I can't tell you what to do. This is like a blank canvas."

Now, for them, this was a radical request. These were blue-collar workers, highly skilled, yes, but since they worked in a paramilitary organization, they fully expected to be told what to do when they came to work. The boss, the foreman, or the superintendent told them what to do and they did it. They had come from an organizational structure of authority that commanded how the whole job was to be done; everyone accepted it. What happened next? They looked at me. They looked at the floor. I sat there.

Silence. I sat there and waited for them to come up with some concepts, ideas, movements. Silence. They really didn't believe that they were taken off the job to sit in this hut with some artist who was running this project and not be told what to do. We sat there. Inside my head, the meter was running, ticking loudly, and a voice was whispering, do something! This is day one with only three days more for creating the whole work. Thirty-two yawning blocks of Madison Avenue— waiting. I had already worked for months to get to this point. Then I said to myself, "Keep your mouth shut. Don't say a word. They need to see that you mean it, that you want the ideas to come from them." Inside, I was shaking. I thought, "Nothing will happen. This will be a colossal failure." We sat there. "Hang in there," I said to myself, "they need to see that you really mean it, that this is something different."

Finally, after an eternity, one of the workers offered an idea. Then another. Then someone said, "No, that won't work, we should do this." It was actually working. Ideas started to fly. They agreed on some things and then really disagreed on others. We got up and went outside. First, they got into their mechanical sweepers and ran through the various capabilities of the vehicles—how the curb brooms and big center broom operated, what the lights did, how their horns and especially how their backup beepers sounded. To me, the backup beepers made a haunting sound and I wanted to incorporate them somehow. That was enough for one day.

The next day, on the first scheduled "rehearsal," we worked the whole day. Our conversation continued all day. They began to try suggestions out. I offered some ideas that I was dying to do. They listened. They smiled and said, "Maybe, but it probably wouldn't work." We tried everyone's ideas out, liked some, and rejected most. Over the next two long full days of rehearsal we began to make decisions. Their skills shined. They sidled right up next to each

other and kissed brooms (which meant that their inner curb brooms almost touched). This was very tricky because they could get entangled with each other's machines and become unbalanced. They were pushing to the edge of what was safe but staying within the rules we had set up: don't tip over and don't run anyone over. Since we would be doing something unusual in front of a lot of people who didn't know what to expect, I became very concerned with the notion of safety, but I also didn't want this to shrink what we could do.

The first deputy commissioner personally had warned me that whatever I planned, no one, *but no one*, is to go backward. Apparently, that was how the vehicle could most likely flip over.[5] I said this again and again during rehearsals and we worked out the entire choreography without anyone going backward.

An element of play bloomed along with their expanding sense of their own authority, as I was fervently hoping for. By then they were pretty charged up. We experimented a lot. I made notes of their everyday work virtues on the street that were showing up within these moves. Some were: flexibility, nerves of steel, ability to deal with anything unexpected popping up, acutely perceiving multiple views from the sweepers' multiple mirrors that enabled them to see everything in the street in all directions all the time (that's how they could kiss brooms), love of fluidity of movement.

The moves we picked and practiced over and over developed an air of inevitability. We made final decisions together and came up with a great series of moves.

PLANNING FOR MOVEMENT III: CEREMONIAL SWEEP

I had heard about an annual Chinese purification ritual that involved work-hierarchy role reversals where the heads of government took over the brooms from street sweepers and hand swept the streets as a measure of respect for those who did this job all year long.

Having been among sanitation workers, I was intensely aware of the sensitivities of differences between the rank and file and everyone above.[6] I wanted to show that those who have the "power of the mouth to speak sanitation" over sanitation workers have a debt of respect to pay to those who have the power of the arm, the hand, the back, and the broom. I wanted to ask them to "do sanitation" as a public gesture of support and evidence of shared responsibility for keeping the city alive.

I launched a campaign to get this particular kind of sweeper for the parade. First, I invited the top tier of authority in the DSNY, including Commissioner Steisel and his entire executive committee. I also invited the presidents of the Uniformed Sanitationmen's Association (the sanitation workers' union) and the Sanitation Officers Association. When I called the workers' union president, Edward Ostrowski, to invite him, he told me he would sweep only on condition that "Norman" would sweep—referring to the commissioner. Because I was desperate to have both, I assured him that Commissioner Steisel would sweep—although, in reality, I had not actually asked him yet. Luckily when I called him, and he immediately asked, "Will Eddy sweep?" I could firmly say, "Yes!" "OK," he said. Whew! Joe Di Masso, president of the officers union, accepted immediately. Then the DSNY executive committee said yes. I had a deal!

Invitations were also sent to city council members, heads of city-oriented foundations, environmental and art-world leaders, so that there would be a full array of "workers." In my letter of invitation to many public officials and notables, I wrote: "As the first Artist-in-Residence in the NYC Department of Sanitation, I would be honored if you would join me and Commissioner Norman Steisel in the 'Ceremonial Sweep' of the First NYC Art Parade. Simply to march? NO! To sweep! This is an ART parade, the first living art parade in NYC's history. This is a performance Maintenance Art Work. This is the Grand Finale."

I also invited members of the press who had written about sanitation workers. In the days of the fiscal crisis in New York City, many members of the media had been brutal, even cruelly contemptuous to sanitation workers, strongly advocating for the city to get rid of DSNY and have sanitation privatized. This had left many wounds among the workers. I was aiming to give these media people a chance to change sides. I wrote:

Commissioner Steisel stressed to me how much he hopes that you and your fellow members of the public media, whose responsibility it is regularly to "talk" and "write" about Sanitation will, on this occasion, be able to "do" together with Sanitation to complete this symbolic—though very real—action with him for this greatest of cities, the international center of art and living artists. He will bring your broom.

Your participation, or that of one of your colleagues, editors, producers, publishers, will exhibit two things: a gesture of honor and support for the regular uniformed sanitation workers who are often

not properly seen and appreciated for a very difficult job, and secondly, as a symbol that maintaining the health of the city is always a "hands-on" societal joint responsibility and ultimately everybody's job. I have asked many many sanitation workers who they would like to see join them in this symbolic action, and they have asked for you.

One reporter, Dennis Duggan, who had written about my earlier work in *New York Newsday*, accepted this invitation.

THE PERFORMANCE IN THREE MOVEMENTS

MOVEMENT I: THE SOCIAL MIRROR

The day of the parade, we were ready to take *The Social Mirror* from the fabrication garage in Brooklyn to Manhattan. A sanitation superintendent had arrived to give the artwork a last inspection, and he got very upset. He realized that the normal separation and looseness between the hopper and body would cause the hopper to bang against the body of the truck and shatter all the glass mirrors by the time it reached Madison Avenue. On his walkie-talkie, he called in a field-welding unit, which showed up immediately. Without a word, right next to the mirrors, they welded the huge hopper to the body of the truck. The welding sparks started a small fire inside the hopper's cavity! But they put it out lickety-split. Their ability to solve unanticipated problems on the spot represented the best of what I revered about DSNY operations. A few minutes later, the truck's body was entirely covered with brown paper and tape, like a giant present, and then covered again with a special heavy canvas, so the mirrors wouldn't disorient drivers as it moved through the streets, hooded like a falcon—and we were on our way to our staging area on Madison Avenue and East 106th Street in Manhattan.

When the dark canvas shield of *The Social Mirror* was lifted off, and then the fitted brown-paper cover

---

5   Because these three-wheeled mechanical sweepers easily became unbalanced, DSNY no longer uses them. Now their fleets of sweepers are all four-wheeled.

6   It reminded me of a story I never forgot from a sanitation worker during *Touch Sanitation* (1977–80). I said to him, "Listen, the officers all come from the ranks. They all started off as sanitation workers just like you. Don't you think that makes them sympathetic to you, to what you need? They were in the same boat as you." "Listen," he answered me, "you know how long it takes the foreman to forget that he was ever a sanitation worker? The time it takes to pick up his officer's pin from the table and bring his arm up to his shoulder and pin it onto his lapel. By the time the pin is in place, he has forgotten all about being a sanitation worker!"

torn off, passersby gasped. People primped in front of their reflection in the truck. When Mayor Ed Koch and Cultural Affairs Commissioner Bess Myerson kicked off the parade, each wearing a *Sanitation Celebrations* button from my work, the excitement around the truck spread by the minute. *The Social Mirror* moved into position, followed by the six mechanical sweepers, followed by all the participants in the *Ceremonial Sweep*.

Streaming slowly straight down the center lane of Madison Avenue, all alone on the street, *The Social Mirror* became something unexpectedly dynamic. Like a movie, it magically split the street in half and played it back as it was passing by, capturing the surprised faces of the viewers lined up along the sidewalks. People cheered.[7]

MOVEMENT II: BALLET MÉCANIQUE FOR SIX MECHANICAL SWEEPERS

We had worked out the following five moves. In my notes I characterized the essence of each move with a name:

Move 1: *Serpentine*
Essence: BEAUTY

Each *serpentine* move took two blocks to play out. The six sweepers divided into pairs and proceeded two by two, moving downtown. This was a statement of ease in taking over the street, a great slowly unfurling line, beginning to curve as it reached the curb edge then turning in a long sinuous diagonal to reach the other curb edge, inside gutter brooms kissing. It was a very tough maneuver and possibly dangerous, because if they came too close together, these two big inner brooms could get entangled in each other and, since these vehicles were three-wheeled and not so well balanced, they could flip each other over. I wasn't worried because I was dealing with such expert pros. The concept of the entire movement was stated immediately from the moment they began their continuous rhythmic curving one way and then the other, as if they were one machine.

Move 2: *Crisscross*
Essence: INTELLIGENCE

The *crisscross*, though at first simple-looking, created an intricate pattern that was different from the *serpentine* in that it was not immediately apparent and devel-

oped only as it played out over a length of two blocks. The six sweepers divided up into two groups of three sweepers. Each group started from opposite sides of the street at the corners. The first set of sweepers on opposite sides started at the same time, on shorter diagonals than the *serpentine*, heading toward each other, passing each other very closely in the center of the street, then kept going toward the curb, turning into another diagonal, and repeated the pattern. Close behind the first set were the second and the third. They synchronized their central passing points from one set of sweepers to the other, so that as all six had entered the move, they were passing each other at the same time. The entire two-block length became so energized by the shifting directionalities and close meetings that they ended up looking as if they were passing *through* each other, almost like a kaleidoscope. It was fascinating to see different gestalts with the same vehicles.

Move 3: *Spider*
Essence: POWER

The *spider* filled the street with sweepers moving in a continually unfolding bellows-like pattern. It had three positions. In the first position, all six sweepers divided themselves into three couples of two sweepers, moving very close to each other, side by side in the center lane. Then they shifted into the second position: one sweeper moved forward to the center of the street alone in front of the other five sweepers. As it moved forward, two sweepers followed that were also in the center of the street and very close together. They were followed by the next two sweepers spreading out sideways, expanding away from each other but keeping in alignment with each other, one to one side of the street and the other to the other side, expanding their lateral spatial pattern maximally. Then they smoothly came back close to each other in the center lane, followed by the last sweeper alone in back of the group in the center of the street. All of this— the moving formation and regrouping in process— occurred as they kept moving downtown. Next came the third position where the sweepers returned back to the first position of three couples close together in the center of the street. They performed this expansion and contraction flying wedge with an incredibly smooth momentum that took one and a half blocks to play out one *spider*.

Move 4: *Face the Audience and Flex Your Muscles*
Essence: JOY

This move was performed by four sweepers on both sides of the street: two sweepers shifted left from their downtown direction, moving perpendicularly, spread out along the block, and came to the curb to directly face the audience standing on the east side of Madison Avenue and stopped. At the same time, two other sweepers shifted right from their downtown direction, moving perpendicularly, spread out along the block, and came to the curb to directly face the audience standing on the west side of Madison Avenue and stopped. Next, all four sweepers did a simultaneous broom routine that consisted of this sequence: lift the hopper, drop rotating curb brooms to the street suddenly, spin the center broom, rotate the curb brooms, then tilt them this way and that, open the cab door, stand up and show yourself to the audience, go back in, back up the sweeper with backup beepers on and lights flashing. Because the ballet consisted of all forward directional momentum up to this point, coming to this stationary perpendicular position was surprising. Before that, most people had never been eye to eye with such a friendly playful sweeping machine that seemed to be calling, perhaps even smiling, and signaling to connect.

Move 5: *Circles and Figure 8s in the Intersections*
Essence: VIRTUOSITY

While the stationary fourth move with four sweepers was going on along the main portion of the block, the other two sweepers moved to the intersections in front of and behind the four other sweepers. The fourth and fifth moves were done at the same time. These two lone sweepers each did tight circles in the center of the block and then, taking over the entire intersection, did multiple figure 8s. Because these three-wheeled vehicles could turn on a dime, the move was performed very fast. The drivers' expertise was altogether dazzling.

However, one young driver, inflamed with inspiration, on his own, did his figure 8s backward in the intersection. Many times. Just my luck! Who is sweeping in the *Ceremonial Sweep* right behind him, completely aghast? The first deputy commissioner, who had my word that no one would do this (and who stopped speaking to me for a long time after that). Thank goodness the sanman didn't tip over.

All five moves of this *ballet mécanique* were repeated every six blocks down the parade route. Thus during the entire thirty-two-block parade, the entire sequence was repeated five times. The Art Parade began near sundown. During the parade the sun had set, and by the end it was night. The moon rose high, crystal clear in the night sky. In the dark, the pulsing lights from *The Social Mirror*'s rear flasher unit and lights from the white sweepers created a kind of light work. The black and white chevrons on the rear of the moving white sweepers with their yellow and red lights blinking and rotating—this was the Constructivist palette come to life. It was getting more and more exciting by the minute. The sanitation drivers were spectacular. It became magical. We sailed down Madison Avenue, owning the street.

MOVEMENT III: CEREMONIAL SWEEP

The full panoply of sanitation authorities, all in business suits, the agency head with members of his executive committee and the heads of both the sanitation workers and officers unions—many of whom were accustomed to facing each other in opposition and sometimes confrontation in the very tough atmosphere across the city's bargaining table—lined up as one team that spanned the street's width, sweeping and sweeping away, following the dancing mechanical brooms. A thrilling group had also accepted this invitation: members from cultural foundations, the media, and the art world all showed personal embodied respect for sanitation workers, out-front in public, going down the street.[8] The significant length of the parade made this task not just a quick cliché of support for labor; thirty-two blocks was long and arduous enough for it to become real. It was a lot of work! The transformation ritual passed an electric message to sanitation workers, some of whom were standing at ease on the sidewalk, some smiling, some open-mouthed, some silent, watching and staring along with other viewers of the parade.

CONCLUSION

This large-scale work, constantly in motion, with the radiant, mesmerizing "mirror truck" floating by, big beeping sweeping machines, twisting, turning, kissing, flowing by—more up close than anyone had experienced—erect people in suits swoosh-swoosh-

7   Since its inception in September 1983 until the present, *The Social Mirror* has been used in parades all over NYC and in many art exhibitions in the city and beyond, see page 49 for details.
8   Their names are listed on page 49.

swooshing their big brooms along, all presented a kind of unbelievable image of "sanitation." A powerful momentum on the street arose as the finale of the parade—which no one had ever seen before in NYC.

AFTER THE PARADE

A sanitation worker in East Brooklyn said to me: "You're like Cézanne: looks simple or crazy and one hundred years later, you realize . . ."

On April 9, 1984, Sanitation Commissioner Norman Steisel wrote to the drivers:

Your expertise, your thorough professionalism and your dedication to this Department and the City mark you as a role model of what "Sanitation" should and can *be. Mierle has told me what a strong and creative leadership role you played in both the design phase and the street ballet implementation—essentially what an artist you are in your work. I'm happy to have this opportunity to tell you how highly I regard your commitment to quality!*

As for the Ballet, I feel you all deserved the lavish media attention, all favorable, that you received. We will never forget it.

The Social Mirror, Columbus Day Parade, 1983

MAINTENANCE ART WORKS

MIERLE LADERMAN UKELES

2-5-79

PROJECT--SANITATION:

"SEE SANITATION -- SEE YOURSELF"
© 1979

Problem:

1. Estrangement of Department of Sanitation (and sanmen) from its public.

2. Inability of public to see its commonality in sharing   *throw out* environmental city-space ---> litter, dirty streets, etc.

Solution:

Mirror the sanitation truck. See the surface of the truck's exterior as the literal interface between the Department and the public. The Sanitation truck does not belong to the Department. It belongs to the public. Mirrored, it reflects the real public space it serves.

Surface is mediator between public service/space (truck) and public served in public space (streets).

Variation 1: whole truck mirrored. Difficulty: will get dirty, graffitti, etc., but can probably be hosed down more effectively than present painted surface-trucks.

Variation 2: certain panels on the sides mirrored.

Note on mirror=material: same kind of industrial mirror material used on skyscrapers: weathers extremely well, very tough, reflective enough to get the idea across, relatively easy maintenance (hosing). Get it donated from manufacturer (new markets!)

Model available shortly.

Original proposal for *The Social Mirror*, 1979

Sanitation research, St. Patrick's Day Parade, 1977

The Social Mirror before the parade, Madison Avenue and 106th Street

Polishing *The Social Mirror* before the parade

Mierle Laderman Ukeles and four of the six drivers
of the mechanical sweepers

Six mechanical sweepers before the parade

Banner constructed from the fabric of sanitation workers' uniforms

DSNY Honor Guard

Ballet Mécanique for Six Mechanical Sweepers

Ballet Mécanique for Six Mechanical Sweepers

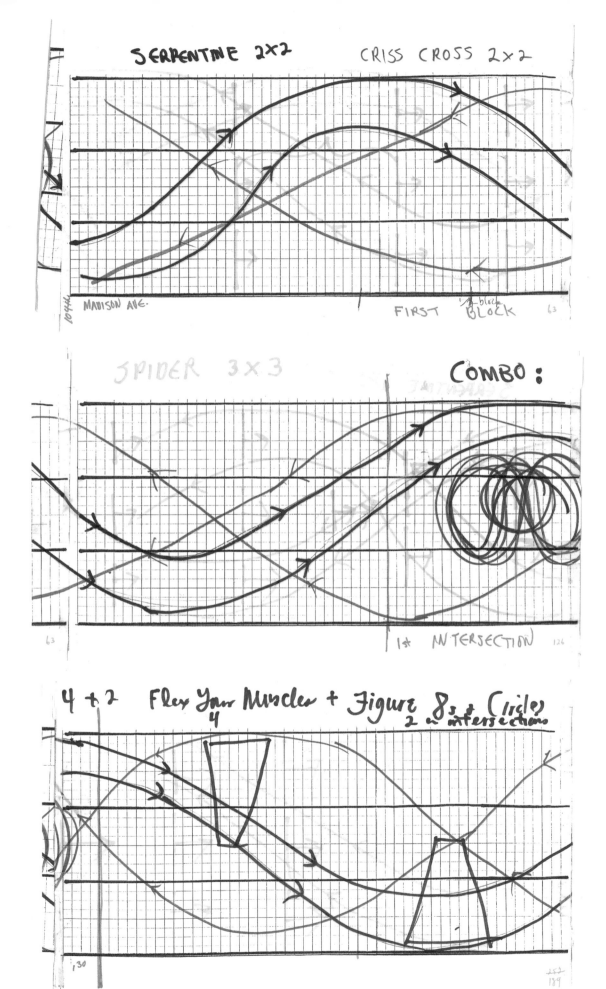

Drawing of choreography, *Ballet Mécanique for Six Mechanical Sweepers*

Ballet Mécanique for Six Mechanical Sweepers

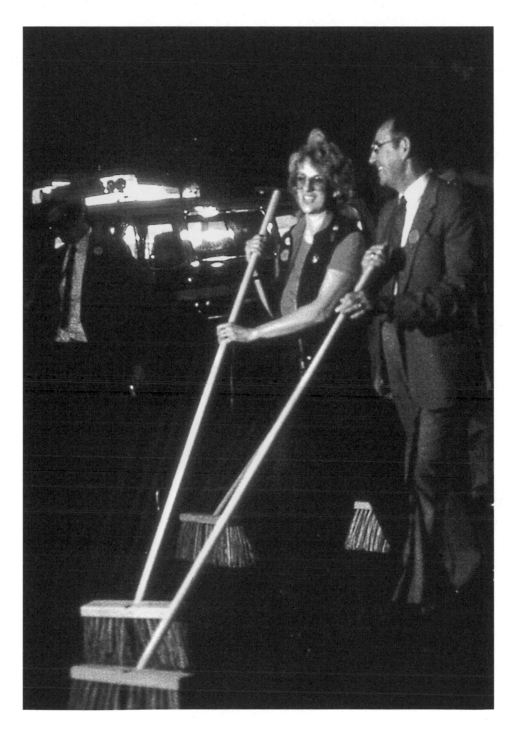

Ceremonial Sweep, Mierle Laderman Ukeles and First Deputy Commissioner
Vincent Whitfield, DSNY

Ceremonial Sweep

CREDITS AND DETAILS

SANITATION CELEBRATIONS
THE GRAND FINALE OF THE FIRST NEW YORK CITY ART PARADE

DATE AND TIME

September 27, 1983
7:00–9:00 p.m.

LOCATION

Manhattan, New York City, United States

SITE

The parade began at East 104th Street and moved south for thirty-two blocks on Madison Avenue to East 72nd Street.

The grand finale staging area was on 105th to 106th Streets on Madison Avenue and on East 105th Street between Fifth and Madison Avenues.

The population of New York City in 1983 was approximately 7,100,000.

INVITING INSTITUTION, STAFF, AND OFFICIALS

First New York City Art Parade:
Henry Korn, Producer and Director

New York City Department of Sanitation (DSNY):
Norman Steisel, Commissioner
Vincent Whitfield, First Deputy Commissioner
Vito A. Turso, Director of Public Information
William Dolan, Deputy Chief of Operations
Blaise Tramazzo, Chief Support Services
Ed Sheridan, Superintendent, Parade Coordinator and presenting official to the New York City Public Design Commission
N. Petito, Foreman

Uniformed Sanitationmen's Association:
Edward Ostrowski, President

Sanitation Officers Association:
Joseph Di Masso, President

Creative Time:
Anita Contini, Founder and Director

New York Foundation for the Arts (NYFA):
Theodore Berger, Executive Director

PROCESSION AND MOVEMENTS

A Maintenance Art Work performance, consisting of:

DSNY Honor Guard
The banner carried by the Honor Guard was made from sanitation workers' uniform material donated by
Antler Uniforms, and fabricated by Bill O'Connor.

Movement I: *The Social Mirror*

The artwork: a twenty-cubic-yard "M series" garbage collection truck with hand-fitted tempered mirrored glass
panels on the flat surfaces and acrylic mirrored panels on the curved areas and vertical structural sections
along the sides. The cab was not mirrored.

Donation of mirrors and other materials for *The Social Mirror* and fabrication and installation costs were
provided anonymously by "a friend who loves New York City"; mirrors fabricated by Colonial Mirror and Glass,
George Weiner. The mirrored panels were installed by Sam Cekic, Brooklyn Glass & Mirror Corp.

Movement II: *Ballet Mécanique for Six Mechanical Sweepers*

The five moves with street lengths:
Serpentine with six sweepers, two blocks
Crisscross with six sweepers, two blocks
Spider with six sweepers, one and a half blocks
Face the Audience and Flex Your Muscles with four sweepers, half a block
Circles and *Figure 8s* with two sweepers in the intersections

Each complete set of the five above moves took six blocks to play out.
All moves were repeated every six blocks.
The complete sets of movements were repeated five times down the thirty-two blocks of the Madison Avenue
parade route.

Movement III: *Ceremonial Sweep*

A work hierarchy and role transformation ritual where organizational leaders took over the brooms, did the
physical act of sweeping, and enabled the sanitation workers to join the rest of the viewers of the parade as
citizens. Brooms were provided by DSNY.

VEHICLES, DRIVERS, AND PERFORMERS

The Social Mirror: a twenty-cubic-yard "M series" garbage collection truck, 23 feet 10 inches long,
5 feet 10 inches wide, and 7 feet high. Chassis by GMC, body by Heil.

Drivers of *The Social Mirror*:
Richard Carr
Michael Cararra

Drivers of the six mechanical sweepers:
Ron Duonola, Bronx W-A
John Fleming, Manhattan West 4A
Nick Habafnick, Queens West 1

John G. Schweikart, Queens West 1
John Siere, Queens West 1
G. Vega, Manhattan East 3A
J. Adamo, Manhattan East 11A (backup driver)

The following people swept thirty-two blocks of the parade route:
Norman Steisel, Commissioner, DSNY
Edward Ostrowski, President, Uniformed Sanitationmen's Association
Joseph Di Masso, President, Sanitation Officers Association
Vincent Whitfield, First Deputy Commissioner, DSNY
Members of the Executive Committee, DSNY
Stanley Michaels, New York City Council Member
Susan Alter, New York City Council Member
Dennis Duggan, reporter, *New York Newsday*
John Coleman, President, Edna McConnell Clark Foundation
Ronald Feldman, Codirector, Ronald Feldman Fine Arts
Anita Contini, Founder and Director, Creative Time
Theodore Berger, Executive Director, NYFA
Lynda Hansen, Director, Artist's Sponsorship Program, NYFA
Mierle Laderman Ukeles

DOCUMENTATION

Video footage (unedited):
Ena Swansea, Videographer
Mark Kaplan, Audio
Melissa Hill, Lighting
NYVAC crew

Photography:
Paula Court
Michael Barbaratto, DSNY
Marita Sturkin

AUDIENCE

The parade was fully barricaded on both sides of the street, at the same level of all major parades
in New York City. Police officers allowed cross streets to pass through periodically, at which time the parade
paused. The audience stood on both sides of Madison Avenue all the way from East 104th Street down
to East 72nd Street.

FURTHER ADVENTURES OF THE SOCIAL MIRROR

The Social Mirror has appeared repeatedly in parades in New York City from 1983 to the present, including
the Pulaski Day Parade, Columbus Day Parade, Halloween Parade, St. Patrick's Day Parade, and Mermaid
Parade. It has been shown in exhibitions including "Touch Sanitation Show, Part One: Transfer Station
Transformation," DSNY West 59th Street Marine Transfer Station, New York, 1984; "Guerrilla Girls at the
Palladium," Palladium, New York, 1985; "Mierle Laderman Ukeles," The Armory Show, Ronald Feldman
Fine Arts, New York, 2007; "Classless Society," The Frances Young Tang Teaching Museum and Art Gallery,
Skidmore College, Saratoga Springs, New York, 2013.

II.

MARRYING THE BARGES:
A BARGE BALLET

OPENING PERFORMANCE OF "TOUCH SANITATION SHOW, PART ONE: TRANSFER STATION TRANSFORMATION"

INTRODUCTION

Marrying the Barges: A Barge Ballet was the only one of my seven work ballets that was not a stand-alone performance. I created it to *initiate* a huge multimedia multilayered project called "Touch Sanitation Show," which took five years to realize and was sited simultaneously in two utterly different locations: a "real" DSNY workplace and an art gallery. I liked the idea of a live performance giving birth to a static installation.

It also, unlike the other six ballets, did not focus primarily on the system's workers. Rather, I created it to illuminate the system itself.

BACKGROUND FOR CREATING A WORK WITH DSNY'S MARINE WASTE DISPOSAL SYSTEM

I admired the marine-based waste disposal system that New York City had designed and operated to gather its waste from all five boroughs and dispose of it at the Fresh Kills Landfill on Staten Island—at 2,200 acres, the largest municipal landfill in the world. This system took advantage of New York City being completely surrounded by waterways, and came from a time when the rivers and harbors were world-class work and transportation networks. It consisted of ten marine transfer stations located on the water's edges. In the marine transfer process, huge, cavernous barges would be hauled by tugboat and delivered to the mouth of the slip—a slender finger of the river—that ran inside the station and served as interior dock. The barge was then pulled into the station by workers expertly manipulating ropes, fed into the special dumping slip, and tied up to receive load upon load of garbage from DSNY garbage trucks dumping the waste from the tipping floor high above. When the barge was fully loaded, the process reversed and the barge, again manipulated by ropes, was "hand-shifted" out of the station, tied up to a waiting tug, and taken many miles for mass disposal at Fresh Kills.

I especially liked this system of marine transfer stations because it was the midpoint between garbage collection and disposal: the two major tasks of waste removal. These were the sites where the garbage entered another zone and seemed to change its nature from being made up of rejected familiar things from one's own life to becoming a "mega flow thing." At this tipping point from truck to barge, these sites became the beginning of scaling up the waste until it became something else, something belonging to the general waste stream. You could still recognize objects, but they were now in flux, merging into a stupendous flow.

All day long, loaded trucks entered the station and backed right up to the curb edge of the tipping floor over the barge slip, guided into place by a sanitation worker who waved his arms like a conductor. Then the trucks lifted their hoppers all the way up almost to the roof of the building. Sometimes many trucks were dumping at the same time and the rhythm of their hoppers rising looked as if they were part of some system-wide composition. Next, each truck's driver engaged the hydraulic packer blade that noisily pushed the waste out. The compressed block of waste emerged slowly and for a moment seemed to halt, poised midair as if it had become one coherent cubic solid, then suddenly lost itself, coming apart in random lurching jags, plunging precipitously into the waiting barge again and again until the truck's cavity was evacuated. Truckload by truckload dropped away until the barge was filled. This was all very theatrical. You could stand there and watch homely objects that you may have just parted with drop abruptly from the hopper of the truck—big objects, like your old friend the couch, broken window frames, a toilet, to tiny objects, coffee grounds, fluttering connected perforated edges of old computer paper, and globs of food remains being stripped of all inherent identities, now joined together into one mass called "garbage"—all falling away in a noisy, crashing, constant flow.

I especially respected this barge system because, though old, it was very ecological. The barges used no fuel. Up to four barges of waste could be tethered together to be hauled by only one tug, which was the only fuel-user in the cluster. Besides not polluting the air from truck fumes, the barges, though transporting multiple truckloads of thousands of tons of waste daily, didn't clog up the city's streets. When four tugs were tied two by two and then tethered to the tug that pulled them, it was called "marrying the barges." They were married; I liked that. The whole smooth operation—the empty barge being delivered, tying up the barge, filling it, sliding it out of the transfer station back to the waiting tug—was a choreography that continued to fascinate me.

Yet this whole daily theatrical enterprise was completely off limits to the public. For years, I had wanted to create a work with the city's marine waste disposal system, to open it up and bring the public in.[1] I searched for a way to create such a work.

"TOUCH SANITATION SHOW": THE CONTEXT FOR THE BARGE BALLET

After years of negotiations and planning with DSNY, I got permission to create and install "Touch Sanitation Show," a kind of Gesamtkunstwerk that would express my years of immersion in New York City's sanitation system as official, unsalaried Artist-in-Residence. By 1984, DSNY devoted the entire August issue of "Open Door," its departmental newsletter published by Public Affairs and distributed to the entire DSNY workforce of about ten thousand people, to the upcoming "Touch Sanitation Show." In Commissioner Norman Steisel's opening article, he cited my description of the exhibition as follows: "A full-scale, total environmental art/work that will celebrate the essential role of maintenance work in our society." He continued: "The show will take place in two distinctly different but equally exceptional locations at the same time—a real sanitation facility and a progressive cultural space—to reflect the often unrecognized interrelationship between work and culture. Mierle wants the SHOW to bridge the unnecessary gulf that separates Sanitation workers from the rest of society by bringing the public into a Sanitation work place and also by exhibiting an expression of the importance of Sanitation work in a place that represents the highest achievements of our urban culture."

"Part One: Transfer Station Transformation," would be the first art exhibition ever held in a real sanitation facility in the United States—the West 59th Street Marine Transfer Station. This pier building on the Hudson River in Manhattan, originally built in 1901, was renovated in 1934 by order of President Franklin Delano Roosevelt and reconstructed by the WPA (Works Progress Administration) during the Great Depression. It was scheduled to be demolished right after the closing of "Touch Sanitation Show," to be replaced by a larger marine transfer station built to handle bigger, taller garbage trucks that could lift their hoppers all the way up without crashing into the roof structure. This performance and exhibition was to be the last hurrah of the old historic station. It would take over the entire sixty-five thousand square feet of the marine transfer station—an installation of many parts to express the reality of DSNY with trucks, barges, landfill equipment, and sanitation workers' voices—to "let them see what it's like here."[2]

"Transfer Station Transformation" included (among other elements), an array of sixteen different kinds of sanitation trucks along the tipping floor positioned over the barge slip, many with their hoppers welded all the way open. I created a two-part sound work, called *Trax for Trux and Barges*, with the sound artist Stephen Erickson, emanating from many concert-grade speakers installed in the barge slip below and also on the ceiling structure overhead. The first sound component was site specific; voices emitted from six of the sixteen trucks on the tipping floor, where the drivers' cabs were empty but many of the trucks were "talking" very frankly from audio-tape interviews I had done with sanitation workers all over New York City. This was to realize a fond wish expressed to me by many sanitation workers: "If only these trucks could talk." So here in this show, they did. The voices alternated in the second part of the sound work with my composition of industrial music from collaged sounds we recorded all over the sanitation system. When this component played, it was as if the entire station was engulfed in, even overwhelmed by the driving mechanical rhythmic sounds of the system.

A steel-mesh trough was suspended in a tipped position halfway between the tipping floor and the barge slip, filled with thousands of dirty, used-up work gloves given to me by individual sanitation workers collected from all over the city during the previous year. (I still meet sanitation workers who tell me, "Hey you have my gloves!" A suspended 350-foot-long light work called *Pulse* made of forty-four flasher units, harvested from defunct garbage trucks, created an energy light that pulsed diagonally all along the station's length. Over the barge slip, I painted a series of *Hand-Energy Flashers*. All of these lights were retrofitted and installed by three kinds of electricians: automotive electricians, high amperage electricians, and house electricians. Across the end wall of the building, six giant steel-mesh containers of separated recyclables rose up from the basement and a hole in the ceiling was cut so that one punctured through the roof. I also cut through the end wall of the station a large saying "No more landfill space / What will we do with all our garbage? Where? How? When? Re —"

THE CONCEPT OF THE PERFORMANCE: WHY A BARGE BALLET?

From the beginning of my concept for this show and throughout its planning, I stressed that this exhibition had to be initiated by a barge ballet. Why? Barges made the place unique. I had been avidly watching tugs and DSNY barges on the city's rivers for seven years. Here was my chance. I asked to work with "the best tugboat captain in the New York Harbor." DSNY agreed.

I met the tugboat captain in the little staff kitchen of the transfer station. He worked for McAllister Bros., the tugboat company that had a contract to haul DSNY garbage barges. I don't know what he had been told about me. I sat at the table facing him. He looked friendly, at ease. This was clearly his domain. "What have you always wanted to do," I asked, "if the coast guard wasn't watching you?" Without skipping a beat, he said, "Make a figure 8 clear across the Hudson River from Manhattan to New Jersey with two barges." OK!

Then he asked, "What's the date?" I told him that the opening of "Touch Sanitation Show" at the marine transfer station site was already scheduled for Sunday, September 9, 1984, from 1:30 p.m. to 2:00 or 2:30 p.m. The time was circumscribed because part two was opening down in SoHo at Ronald Feldman Fine Arts from 3:00 p.m. to 4:00 p.m. that same day!

He took out the tugboat captains' bible: a little white book that shows the tides and their location every day of the year. He checked the tides at the time of the opening and said they would be too choppy for the crisscross necessary to complete a figure 8 at that time on that date. So he offered to create a big, big circle all across the extremely wide Hudson River from Manhattan to New Jersey and back again, hauling two empty barges. I agreed. The meeting had unexpectedly proceeded so smoothly that I forgot to ask his name!

THE PERFORMANCE

On September 9, the audience stood along the entire specially built 350-foot-long fence on the tipping floor of the old West 59th Street Marine Transfer Station, with most gathering at the river end to watch the ballet.[3]

1   This desire to open up the system and to bring the public in found initial expression in my 1983 concept for *Flow City*, proposed as a permanent environmental public artwork to be built for the new West 59th Street Martine Transfer Station. It was half built but is currently on hold while the DSNY waste disposal system is being redesigned since the closure of Fresh Kills Landfill in 2001.
2   The second simultaneous part of the exhibition, "Maintenance City/Sanman's Place," would be a one-person installation at Ronald Feldman Fine Arts in SoHo, with an initiating performance outside on Mercer Street.
3   Since this building was never built for public access, it took many meetings with city officials and consulting engineers to determine that this old facility would be safe for a big audience. To ensure everyone's safety, the Department of Sanitation built and installed a fence and guardrail all along the tipping floor especially for this show.

Marrying the Barges: A Barge Ballet had two movements. The first movement was the passage by the transfer station of four married barges that had been fully loaded with garbage at a transfer station upriver, pulled by one tug. I wanted to establish an image of everyday reality. Just as what normally happened on the river, approximately 2,500 tons of municipal waste, tethered together, glided by the station and disappeared down the Hudson River.

The second movement was not usual. The captain, piloting his tug, appeared in front of the transfer station in full view of the audience. He was pulling two empty barges, a beat-up old barge and a brand-new blue and orange barge, with the old one in the front. Sure enough, the captain, keeping them in a perfectly spaced line, led them in a circle that began at the station and arced all across the Hudson River, cutting across the choppy tide, to New Jersey, then arced back again to Manhattan, completing the huge circle. The writer for "Talk of the Town" in the *New Yorker* described them in the issue of September 24, 1984: "Soon the barges, which were empty of garbage, were doing glissades out in the Hudson, and they seemed to be enjoying themselves." Then, in the final moments of the ballet, the tug guided the old and the new barges seamlessly and silently into the mouth of the barge slip, and nudged them in, and released them. The transfer station's onshore crew took over, reeling out thick bright-white ropes, pulled the barges along until they filled up the slip, and tied them up beneath the audience, who were standing on the tipping floor high above, next to and in between several garbage trucks, which were busy "talking away" though carrying no driver nor any garbage, with their hoppers extended all the way up, welded open over the empty barges.

I was always awed by the yawning, clear space within the empty barges. Side by side in the slip below, they were like a double-barreled minimalist sculpture: two enormous hollow rectangles, deeper than one imagined. Waiting. The writer for the *New Yorker* concluded: "We leaned over the railing and peered down into the cavern of the barge . . . it looked vast and deep and patient."

Movement I: Four DSNY barges loaded with New York City garbage, married to each other and moving south on

the Hudson River

Movement II: Beginning to make a circle across the Hudson River

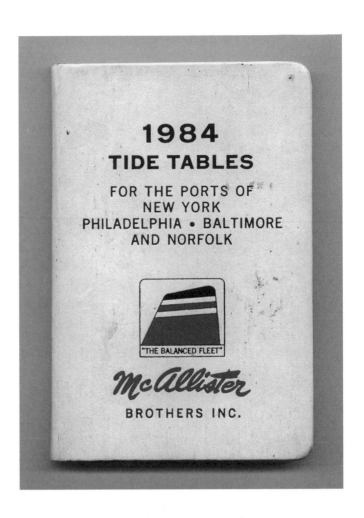

1984
TIDE TABLES
FOR THE PORTS OF
NEW YORK
PHILADELPHIA • BALTIMORE
AND NORFOLK

"THE BALANCED FLEET"

McAllister
BROTHERS INC.

EASTERN STANDARD TIME — CURRENT TABLE, SEPTEMBER 1984

DAY	DATE	EAST RIVER High Water Slack		EAST RIVER Low Water Slack		NORTH RIVER High Water Slack		NORTH RIVER Low Water Slack	
S	1	01.56	14.28	07.46	20.39	02.46	15.18	09.06	21.59
S	2	02.52	15.26	08.51	21.50	03.42	16.16	10.11	23.10
M	3	03.54	16.25	10.02	22.58	04.44	17.15	11.22	....
T	4	04.58	17.30	11.05	23.55	05.48	18.20	00.18	12.25
W	5	05.56	18.30	12.02	....	06.56	19.20	01.15	13.22
T	6	06.57	19.25	00.46	12.54	07.57	20.15	02.06	14.14
F	7	07.57	20.10	01.34	13.44	08.47	21.00	02.54	15.04
S	8	08.40	20.53	02.19	14.30	09.30	21.43	03.39	15.50
S	9	09.19	21.31	03.01	15.12	10.09	22.21	04.21	16.32
M	10	09.54	22.06	03.39	15.52	10.44	22.56	04.59	17.12
T	11	10.30	22.40	04.15	16.29	11.20	23.30	05.35	17.49
W	12	11.05	23.11	04.47	17.02	11.55	....	06.07	18.22
T	13	11.36	23.41	05.15	17.34	00.01	12.26	06.35	18.54
F	14	12.05	....	05.39	18.03	00.31	12.55	06.59	19.23
S	15	00.07	12.37	05.59	18.32	00.57	13.27	07.19	19.52
S	16	00.42	13.14	06.21	19.09	01.32	14.04	07.41	20.29
M	17	01.27	13.59	06.53	20.17	02.17	14.49	08.13	21.37
T	18	02.20	14.56	07.45	22.04	03.10	15.46	09.05	23.24
W	19	03.27	16.24	09.26	23.14	04.17	16.54	10.46	....
T	20	04.51	17.23	11.11	....	05.41	18.13	00.34	12.31
F	21	06.10	18.33	00.09	12.14	07.00	19.23	01.29	13.34
S	22	07.12	19.31	01.00	13.10	08.02	20.21	02.20	14.30
S	23	07.55	20.23	01.48	14.05	08.55	21.13	03.08	15.25
M	24	08.52	21.10	02.37	14.56	09.42	22.00	03.57	16.16
T	25	09.38	21.59	03.23	15.47	10.28	22.49	04.43	17.07
W	26	10.27	22.48	04.07	16.35	11.17	23.38	05.27	17.55
T	27	11.17	23.42	04.52	17.25	12.07	....	06.12	18.45
F	28	12.12	....	05.36	18.13	00.32	13.02	06.56	19.33
S	29	00.39	13.06	06.21	19.09	01.29	13.56	07.41	20.29
S	30	01.35	14.03	07.16	20.12	02.25	14.53	08.36	21.32

East River slack water lasts from 4 to 8 minutes. North River about 35 minutes. North River is running flood 15 feet below the surface 1 hour before turning from ebb to flood at surface. High water slack occurs in the Narrows 15 minutes before the H.W.S. East River and low water slack occurs about 20 minutes before the L.W.S. North River.

EASTERN STANDARD TIME — TIDE TABLE, SEPTEMBER 1984

DATE	SANDY HOOK High Water		SANDY HOOK Low Water		THE BATTERY High Water		THE BATTERY Low Water	
1	12.17	....	05.54	18.39	00.26	12.58	06.26	19.19
2	00.38	13.13	06.53	19.46	01.22	13.56	07.31	20.30
3	01.37	14.14	07.59	20.53	02.24	14.55	08.42	21.38
4	02.44	15.17	09.01	21.51	03.28	16.00	09.45	22.35
5	03.53	16.19	10.00	22.46	04.36	17.00	10.42	23.26
6	04.56	17.15	10.54	23.36	05.37	17.55	11.34	....
7	05.47	18.01	11.44	....	06.27	18.40	00.14	12.24
8	06.27	18.42	00.19	12.32	07.10	19.23	00.59	13.10
9	07.05	19.19	01.01	13.16	07.49	20.01	01.41	13.52
10	07.42	19.56	01.42	13.58	08.24	20.36	02.19	14.32
11	08.16	20.30	02.18	14.35	09.00	21.10	02.55	15.09
12	08.48	21.04	02.51	15.10	09.35	21.41	03.27	15.42
13	09.23	21.39	03.22	15.44	10.06	22.11	03.55	16.14
14	09.55	22.13	03.49	16.16	10.35	22.37	04.19	16.43
15	10.33	22.52	04.16	16.50	11.07	23.12	04.39	17.12
16	11.13	23.38	04.48	17.35	11.44	23.57	05.01	17.49
17	12.01	....	05.24	18.39	12.29	....	05.33	18.57
18	00.33	12.57	06.25	19.57	00.50	13.26	06.25	20.44
19	01.38	14.06	07.48	21.07	01.57	14.34	08.06	21.54
20	02.53	15.17	09.05	22.05	03.21	15.53	09.51	22.49
21	04.07	16.25	10.09	22.59	04.40	17.03	10.54	23.40
22	05.07	17.26	11.07	23.51	05.42	18.01	11.50	....
23	06.00	18.17	12.05	....	06.35	18.53	00.28	12.45
24	06.49	19.06	00.41	12.59	07.22	19.40	01.17	13.36
25	07.35	19.54	01.30	13.52	08.08	20.29	02.03	14.27
26	08.21	20.41	02.16	14.42	08.57	21.18	02.47	15.15
27	09.10	21.31	03.02	15.31	09.47	22.12	03.32	16.05
28	10.02	22.24	03.47	16.21	10.42	23.09	04.16	16.53
29	10.53	23.17	05.34	17.41	11.36	....	05.01	17.49
30	11.48	....	05.25	18.12	00.05	12.33	05.56	18.52

Slack water at Sandy Hook occurs 50 minutes after H.W. and 1 hour and 10 minutes after L.W. and lasts about 25 minutes

F.Q. 2   F.M. 10   L.Q. 18   N.M. 24

East River Constant   HWS Batt. +1:30   LWS Batt. +1:20
North River Constant   HWS Batt. +2:20   LWS Batt. +2:40

The tide book used by the tugboat captain to determine possible choreography

Movement II: Feeding the old and new barge into the marine transfer station slip

NO MORE LANDFILL —

WHERE?

Movement II: New and old barge stationed in the slip under the garbage trucks

CREDITS AND DETAILS

MARRYING THE BARGES: A BARGE BALLET
OPENING PERFORMANCE OF "TOUCH SANITATION SHOW, PART ONE:
TRANSFER STATION TRANSFORMATION"

DATE AND TIME

September 9, 1984
1:30–2:30 p.m.

LOCATION

Manhattan, New York City, United States

SITE

The ballet took place in the DSNY West 59th Street Marine Transfer Station and on the Hudson River.

The population of New York City in 1984 was approximately 7,100,000.

INVITING INSTITUTION, STAFF, AND OFFICIALS

New York City Department of Sanitation (DSNY):
Norman Steisel, Commissioner
Vito A. Turso, Director of Public Information and Community Affairs

Creative Time:
Anita Contini, Founder and Director

Ronald Feldman Fine Arts:
Ronald and Frayda Feldman, Codirectors

New York Foundation for the Arts (NYFA):
Theodore Berger, Executive Director
Lynda Hansen, Director, Artist's Sponsorship Program

MOVEMENTS

Movement I: Four DSNY barges loaded with New York City garbage, a symbol of everyday reality,
were married to each other and pulled by a tug that passed by the audience, moving south past the audience
on its way to disposal at the Fresh Kills Landfill.

Movement II: Two empty barges, an old one and a new one, tied to a tug that pulled them in a huge circle
clear across the Hudson River, arching from New York to New Jersey and back again, then fed them into
the mouth of the barge slip at the transfer station as the audience watched. They were then tied up in the slip
and "Touch Sanitation Show" was initiated.

BOATS AND BARGES

Additional information from DSNY Public Information and former DSNY officials from 1984:
Size of a DSNY barge: 140 feet long, 15 feet wide, and 37.5 feet deep.
Number of average garbage truckloads to fill up a barge: sixty to sixty-five.
In 1984, the carrying capacity of each DSNY barge was approximately 600 to 650 tons. Thus, the four loaded DSNY barges in the first movement of the *Barge Ballet* transported about 2,500 tons of waste to Fresh Kills Landfill.

DOCUMENTATION

Photography:
Jennifer Kotter
Andrew Moore
D. James Dee

AUDIENCE

They stood all along the edge of the barge slip's 350 foot-long tipping floor, secured by a mesh fence and guardrail that DSNY had built especially for the exhibition. Most gathered at the western end of the station at the mouth of the barge slip in order to watch the barges' arrival.

III.

VUILNISWAGENDANS (GARBAGE TRUCK DANCE)

INVITATION

In 1984, out of the blue, I was invited to "appear" at the festival Perfo 3 by curator Wink van Kempen and Fred van der Hilst, director of the LantarenVenster Cultural Center in Rotterdam. They called the "manifestation" a "festival for the art of appearances" with the title "Een Soort Schoonheid / A Kind of Beauty."

Rotterdam was especially interesting to me because it was a powerful, highly industrial city with the world's busiest working harbor at that time. I imagined that the value of physical labor was supreme here and retained a kind of elan that it lacked in other less work-oriented cities. I was also eager to work outside New York City, my hometown, to show that the subjects of maintenance and the importance of service workers were universal wherever there are cities. I felt I could go to any city anywhere in the world and get to work right away. Doing a piece here could prove it.

I accepted the invitation and sent Van Kempen a cluster of early proposals. Captivated by the huge scale of Rotterdam's working harbor knitted right into the city, I wanted to do a work that occurred simultaneously in the city and in the harbor's water at the port.

GOING INTERNATIONAL: BUILDING TRANSNATIONAL SUPPORT

Siting my work within the city's infrastructure, including its great harbor, was different from the interests of the other festival participants, who were proposing smaller-scale works, mostly staying within the theater inside the cultural center. Intent on separating my "real" performance work from the very notion of theater, I felt I had to reach out beyond the work sited indoors, so people from the world of infrastructure work who had never heard of me might find a way to trust me and allow me to enter and engage their dangerous work environments.

My need to build a unique and broad working coalition grew out of my conceptualization of the meaning of being Artist-in-Residence in the DSNY. I regarded my presence there not only as relating specifically to New York City, but rather as a conceptual platform from which I could deal with a global idea of the environment, including "sanitation," as being supranational and omnipresent, not simply located in one place. Further, the DSNY itself was already working with people and companies internationally to explore bringing newly developing technologies for waste disposal to New York City. So the next day, I enlisted the help of Paul Casowitz, the DSNY Deputy Commissioner for Resource Recovery and Waste Disposal Planning, since I had learned that some of the companies he dealt with had European branches in and close to Rotterdam. I asked for his help in making these contacts for me and also to ask him to make a peer-to-peer connection for me with the head of the sanitation department in Rotterdam. Deputy Commissioner Casowitz wrote to the heads of the two largest international resource-recovery companies that he dealt with, who also had offices in Rotterdam and nearby cities, to introduce me and my interests.[1] He agreed to try to leverage the support of leaders in the waste-recovery system who were already connected to the sanitation department in Rotterdam in order to build their confidence in my work. In support of this, Casowitz wrote to them: "A word to ease any caution, since I know this is unusual . . . She is able to work with

---

1   "Resource recovery" is the technical name given to alternative waste-disposal technologies prominent in the 1980s, where thermal energy from incinerating garbage at a very high heat is captured, cleaned by the addition of pollution-destroying technologies, and utilized as new energy. These plants were quite common in European cities, but still new and rather controversial as a method of waste disposal in the United States at the time.

all kinds of workers and managers in very restrictive and even dangerous work environments." Casowitz asked Gloria Mills, vice president of Ogden Martin, to contact their Munich office to put in a good word about me to Rotterdam. She followed up, then suggested that Van Kempen and I make contact with T. H. Kros, director of the Rotterdam sanitation department, who had already heard from Ogden Martin's Munich office, and was expecting to hear from me. Buoyed by these multiple levels of support, I wrote to Mr. Kros directly in hope of "collaborating" with him and the City of Rotterdam's Department of Sanitation and sent him a hugely ambitious multipart proposal, including:

I. *"Follow In Your Footsteps."* For several days, spending the entire workday with several crews, following one worker at a time, *"like a phantom,"* copying his every movement in *"a dance of work."* . . . *"If the worker agrees, I will tie myself to him, of course with enough length between us not to interfere with the work, with mountain-climbing equipment: pulleys, springs, ropes, etc. These ties symbolize life and death dependence and trust."*

II. *"Machine Dance On Land And Sea."* Or could be called *"Ballet Mécanique [sic].* This would be a three act Ballet (or two act Ballet).

ACT I: Machine Dance On Land . . . A Machine Dance with garbage trucks and / or mechanical sweepers, if you have them . . . with the best drivers you have. For a public square, arena or streets."

ACT II: Barge Ballet: to celebrate your great harbor and the fact that yours (along with New York City and, I think, Geneva) are the only barge-fed waste-disposal systems in the world."

Sound Component
I want to include sound from resource recovery plants . . . and play these sounds as part of this Ballet, through speakers, either on the Barges or around the area of the Ballet.
The idea of this Sound Component is that you, the Sanitation Department, take the garbage away. At the Resource Recovery plant, the garbage gets transformed to energy: steam and electricity which is returned to the City, *"almost like ghosts of the garbage, reincarnated, returned "to life." I want to make audible the energy returned, the sound of transformation back to the City."*

ACT III: Truck & Barge Ballet
Is there a point, an area at the harbor, perhaps at the transfer point, where the trucks and the barges meet? So that collection and disposal can be expressed in the Ballet. Land and Sea meet, etc.

CONCLUSION

The purpose of these projects is to celebrate everyday maintenance of the city's life. You all keep the city a living entity with your unending labor . . . This art is a very functional and respectful philosophy of culture that says: everyday work is filled with reality, creativity and enduring wisdom. People know this INSIDE the work system. The maintenance artist serves as a lens and as a bridge to let this BEAUTY OUT, so the general public can see it and appreciate it.

On a deeper level, it asks a utopian question. I don't know the answer, but I long to ask it anyway:

Can work, necessary work, ever be so harmonious and respectful of the fullness of capability of humanity that it runs seamlessly into art? If we set it up right, can everyday life ever be full of the highest level of meaningfulness and beauty? . . .

I know I am asking a lot from you and your whole system. I am certainly willing to adjust all of the above and to work out a DO-Able project. THE ABOVE IS NOT SET IN STONE . . . It can certainly be adjusted . . . I look forward, very much, to working with you.

FIRST MEETINGS WITH OFFICIALS

I had never been to the Netherlands before I arrived in Rotterdam in May 1985, but I felt as if I knew a lot about the country, having been well taught by Rembrandt and Van Gogh, among lots of other Dutch painters. As I came in from the airport, I recognized the landscape I saw from my train window from Van Gogh. Early the next morning I met with Van Kempen, Hubert Kros, the Director of the Sanitation Department (ROTEB); his First Deputy for Operations, J. C. Kalisvaart; and Jahn van Rijn, Media and Education Director. Kros gave me two neckties for the DSNY commissioners in New York City and an umbrella; then we got down to business. They were very positive. After several prior phone calls between Van Kempen, the local European representative of Ogden Martin, and Kros, the sanitation department had accepted two of my proposals and had already worked out many details with Van Kempen. The city would provide a large rectangular public square in West Rotterdam called Visserijplein (Fisheries Market) for a ballet of six garbage trucks and four mechanical sweepers that would conclude with a procession through the city to the festival center. They also agreed to produce my idea of a resource-recovery sound work with Van Rijn, which would be broadcast, not on barges, but in the square during the ballet.

To my great regret, I could not get anyone that I met in the sanitation department to deal with the harbor at all, even though I felt the working harbor signified Rotterdam and would be natural for this work. So, despite my logic, it never made it out the door. Since I was there for such a short time, I needed to focus only on what was at least possible. I told myself, another day for the harbor. The other proposal for "Follow in Your Footsteps" also was not considered.

AND THE DRIVERS

I had asked to meet with drivers of garbage trucks and street sweepers. A large roomful of drivers waited to meet me in another area of the same building. All the drivers had blue eyes. I had the incredible sensation, while looking out across the meeting room filled with so many drivers looking back at me, that I was looking at the ocean in the summer. I already knew their names from art history: Terborch, Van Rijn. I told them about my earlier work and showed them slides of artworks with other maintenance workers, hoping they would see that I highly respected this kind of work and had also gained some expertise in their work mission and techniques. Like the very first time I had met with New York City sanitation workers to create a ballet for the 1983 Art Parade, I was terrified.

There was a lightness of spirit and exuberance among the workers in the room during this first meeting that I had not encountered before. Things looked promising. In that room we started to come up with ideas for movements right away. I explained that I wasn't there to tell them what to do. My main idea was that we would do this together; they enthusiastically agreed. I stressed that I was very interested in the power of their imagination!

However, one of the bosses of the drivers, who had been extremely helpful in getting me started, became fixated on the ballet. His intense involvement, spoken loudly in his customary authoritative boss voice, began to impinge on the workers' imagination and damage my whole working theory of everyone being equally empowered. He said things like, "We must

do this and then we'll do that." The second day of rehearsal, he came in with movement designs he liked and just assumed that we would do them. I felt the overall spirit of the work slipping away. I didn't know how to deal with him. As he was getting more and more excited, the workers were getting more silent and withdrawn. Then, the next morning, he called me at my hotel, very early in the morning, and said that unfortunately his back went out and he couldn't even get out of bed; I would have to carry on without him. After commiserating with him, I breathed a sigh of relief. I must admit that he had contributed some very clever ideas; we kept his idea for the movement he called the *carousel*, but we did it because we jointly chose it. We were able to move forward—liberated!—with everyone's ideas on the table.

Early on, something unexpected tipped me off to the extraordinary position of sanitation workers in Rotterdam: the great architectural design of their workplace. The facilities they showed me that first day and the place where we had lunch every day afterward revealed a level of respect toward the workers that I had never seen in sanitation facilities in New York City or London! Here were waxed wooden floors, big windows in the lunchroom with what looked like Alvar Aalto furniture and modernist drapes, hot catered meals for lunch, songbirds in cages, and, incredibly, individual lockers that had two sections: a heated section to hold your wet raincoat when you came in for lunch so it would be dry when you went back out again, and an unheated section for your regular clothes! When I saw that, I almost fainted. Clearly the city was very attentive to its workers. I imagined that they were extremely well organized as a labor force.

Every day for the rest of that week and the beginning of the next week we went to Visserijplein and worked. We measured all the trucks and saw all the moves they could do. Little by little we came up with many possible moves, and I drew diagrams of them. The fact that Visserijplein was a public square that also became a big market twice a week (except during our rehearsals), but was also set in the midst of a residential neighborhood, had an impact on our work. People who lived in Visserijplein were simply around much of our time, especially kids. They watched us from the first moment we arrived to rehearse in "their" space and sort of got used to us. By the time of the performance itself, we had developed a local audience, a very enthusiastic one, besides the many fresh new visitors who arrived just for the performance from the festival and beyond.

SOUND WORK
COLLECTION FROM THE FIELD AND
COMPOSITION

Meanwhile, in between rehearsals, I began work with Jahn van Rijn, collecting sound to accompany the ballet. We made field recordings that tracked the sounds of garbage being transformed into electricity and steam, selected from walking throughout the ROTEB system and from our visit to the Ogden Martin plant, a barge-fed resource-recovery plant in Rotterdam that handled 999 tons of waste per day. I described some of the sounds in my field notes: "Air brakes, back up, open hopper, dump; crane lifting material going from down to up, repeat and repeat; close the door [of the incinerator]; destructor boom chopping the wood, wood 'crying' as it is crushed; twinkling ashes falling, twinkling, and metal dropping; conveyor belt and puff pipes; seagulls." We assembled these sound bits into a collaged composition, and this became the main audio part of the ballet.

CREATION AND REHEARSALS

We had four long days of rehearsals leading up to the day of the performance, Wednesday, May 15. The long square, eighty-six meters long and sixty-five meters wide, was surrounded on all four sides by the flat, dull surfaces of connected dark-gray buildings, pierced by a few narrow openings for street entrances. This simple large "stage," a virtually encapsulated rectilinear prism, made the precise geometry of the vehicles' fluid movements very clear, even intensely minimalist. Each move became lucid from every point of view. The formal drama unfolding in this enclosed space was increased by the size differences between six very large lumbering white garbage trucks in relation to four tiny, almost toylike, white sweepers. Both had yellow and red lights circling and flashing. The city had made huge posters announcing the *Vuilniswagendans* as well, and they covered a large portion of the sides of the big garbage trucks.

THE PERFORMANCE

Before the performance, I distributed a packet of diagrams of all the moves to each driver with the following note:

Dear Roteb Friend: "Vuilnisman,"
Here are the basic diagrams of the Vuilniswagendans. *We made this dance together! Working with you has been like a beautiful dream. Thank you.*
Let's make it all come true tonight. Good luck!
Your friend always,
Mierle Ukeles

It was getting dark. Before the ballet began, I walked around the square greeting and shaking hands with many members of the audience.

MOVEMENT I
FOLLOW THE LEADER

The ballet began with an empty stage. No trucks were present in the square; they were lined up in a narrow street that opened directly onto it. At a signal, the drivers turned on their motors, creating a big sound, and the sound work started playing, permeating the space with a popular song that most people knew, called "Ich bin ein vuilnisman" (I am a garbage collector). On signal, the six big garbage trucks appeared, lights twirling and flashing! They entered single file, followed by the four tiny sweepers, also single file. Following the straight lines of the building facades, they made a hard charging procession twice along the perimeter, mirroring the entire rectangular space.

MOVEMENT II
SNAKE: LONG SNAKE, MINI SNAKE,
CRISSCROSS

The straight lines turned into a slow-moving, sinuous and continuous *long snake*: traversing the space from one side of the square to the other, then turning in a tight radius to switch directions with the garbage trucks doubling up into three groups of two trucks and the sweepers still following, doubling up into two groups of two. They drove very close to each other. This was followed by a *mini snake* where the snake's continuous long twisting and curving line constricted to the center of the square in very tight switches, then split at the end of the line, with every other truck alternating—one going to the right and one going to the left, out toward and then along the perimeter, straight down—to meet again in the center to double up once again to form tight twisting switches. The movement shifted from wide and slowly winding to very tight, quick, and contained, and looked surprisingly organic!

The final segment of the *snake* was called *crisscross*, where the garbage trucks followed by the sweepers divided into two groups, each starting from an opposite corner of the square. They made five diagonal zigzag crossings in a harlequin pattern, passing right next to each other in the center by a hair's breadth, then heading to the outer edges, turning sharply, and repeating the pattern. The *crisscross* ended with the sweepers lining up at the narrow end of the square (in preparation for the next movement) while the garbage trucks, dividing into two groups of three, repeated the sharp diagonal pattern of the *crisscross*, only this time in single file.

MOVEMENT III
THE SEA LIONS HUNT THE HERRINGS

Everyone I had talked to in New York before my trip urged that while in Rotterdam, I had to make sure to eat the freshest herrings in the world, right out of the barrel. I told the drivers this story. We started talking about the precarious lives of herrings. Out of this came the hide-and-seek game we called *The Sea Lions Hunt the Herrings*. This move had the excitement of a children's chase ritual. Five garbage trucks (sea lions), silent and still at one end of the square, faced four tiny sweepers (herrings) that faced them far away at the other end of the square. The sixth garbage truck, the vicious hunter sea lion, alone, slowly sneaked forward, inching along the very long edge of the square. Slowly the big and the little trucks advanced toward each other until they met in the center and then each little sweeper-herring sought shelter in between the nearest friendly hovering garbage trucks. They were hiding there when suddenly the hunter sea lion made his move and swerved sharply in front of all the trucks, searching for herrings. Frantic, the herrings darted loose, escaping in erratic wiggle-waggle wobbly lines, and dashed to the other end of the square. Then the herring sweepers turned around in happiness and found the wicked sea lion waiting for them again, so the whole drama was repeated all over again.

MOVEMENT IV
TEN MAKE EIGHT AND TRANSITION

The garbage trucks took a position at each corner of the square and also at the midpoint along the square's long sides. The four sweepers formed a straight line, close together, in the center of the square. Each was silent and still. Suddenly, all ten trucks made tight figure 8s in place. The whole space was filled with twirling trucks.

Then, while the garbage trucks continued turning, the sweepers moved into a transition pattern by turning their straight line into an inner circle. This was followed by each of the six garbage trucks peeling off, one at a time, to form a larger circle around the sweepers.

MOVEMENT V
CAROUSEL

This led to the *carousel*, the most complex movement, where the garbage trucks then peeled off out of the center circle toward the right and created another circle at one end of the square, did one complete circle, then fed back into the larger center circle, made two rotations, then peeled off toward the left and created another circle at the opposite end of the square, made two rotations, then came back to the center for two more rotations. All the while, the sweepers stayed within the center circle and continued their own tight circling. The continual expansion and spiraling outward and back in was almost dizzying and was performed perfectly.

FINALE

PART I: HOPPER CANCAN
(FOR THE GARBAGE TRUCKS)

All ten trucks spread out and lined up in the middle of the square with the six garbage trucks with their hoppers along the center line in the middle and the sweepers at the ends, two and two. Everyone honked. The sweepers stayed still, with lights turning, like bookends. The garbage trucks proceeded to do a *cancan* in three different sequential moves. First, all lifted their hoppers together two times. Secondly, they did the "stairs," where each truck in sequence lifted its hopper a bit higher than the one before, with the sixth lifting its hopper all the way up—then reversed and repeated. And finally, the *cancan* concluded with the garbage trucks creating a simultaneous stepped pyramid, which they called "the bird," with the two end trucks lifting just a bit, the next two trucks in lifting a little more, and then the two center trucks lifting their hoppers all the way up. They held this ziggurat shape, then reversed and repeated it. Altogether, these three moves, performed seamlessly one after the other, made it look like a wave of hoppers had overtaken the trucks.

PART II: BROOM DANCE
(BORSTELDANS, FOR THE SWEEPERS)

Mechanical sweepers are commonly called "brooms" because of their rotating brooms that are flexible and can raise up and tip one way and then the other. The four mechanical sweepers left the garbage trucks, forming a kind of wall in the back, and stayed still and silent throughout this whole move. The tiny sweepers came forward—two from one side of the garbage trucks and two from the other—lining up in the middle of the square. I stepped forward, faced them, and, in an unplanned movement of my own, conducted the *Broom Dance* as if they were players in an orchestra. Their stationary brushes were down. Together they began to rotate faster and faster. Next the sweepers raised up a bit on their haunches, and their brushes swung left and out, then right and out. This sequence was repeated three times. The sudden shift in movement scale, switching from the waving of the giant hoppers to the swinging moves of these small, round, cute brushes, was charming and intimate. The move ended with the sweepers lifting their hoppers. Then we repeated the whole sequence, facing three different sides of the square.

A lovely thing developed as part of the *Broom Dance* with the little sweepers. There were many little children in the audience who had been following us each day of the rehearsals. As we moved the sweepers to repeat this dance sequence on the three sides of the square—moving the trucks to bring them up close to different sections of the audience—several of these kids just trooped along with me and we ended up all conducting together! The ballet had become theirs.

The finale concluded with all the drivers getting out of their vehicles and taking a bow. Then they joined the audience for a community sing of "Laat het niet verder meer gaan" (Don't let it go on),[2] a popular environmental song distributed to all the drivers and members of the audience. People loved it and we belted it out at the top of our lungs!

As promised, the sound system provided by the city during the ballet was first rate, with equipment used for outdoor concerts—so the sound work reverberated throughout the space of the Visserijplein for the duration of the performance. It began with the popular garbage-collector song and continued with the sound collage of resource-recovery industrial music that Van Rijn and I had composed, keyed to different movements of the ballet. Van Kempen stood with me in the midst of the dance. At the end, he turned to me and said, "I'm in the middle of Futurism! The original Futurists would be so happy tonight."

The sanitation workers were fabulous! They had no hesitation about having members of their own families ride in the trucks with them during the ballet. The dynamic momentum unleashed in each movement, which coursed from one movement to the next, reflected their awesome skill and unique, unstoppable, high-spirited sense of play. There was an enormous feeling of elation and release among both the audience and the drivers at the completion of the ballet as we all went in a procession to the festival's cultural center to celebrate.

I think my intuition was correct about Rotterdam setting a special context for this work. The predominance of heavy industry made this a muscular city where respect for labor was embedded in their citizens' sense of reality. That rubbed off on the way the general population saw and valued the sanitation workers and the way the sanitation workers saw themselves and valued their service to the city. Together they showed how a high level of connectedness between the municipal service workers and the citizens made the whole urban enterprise vivacious, playful, and wise.

AFTER THE PERFORMANCE

When I returned home, I wrote to Gloria Mills, my contact at Ogden Martin who connected me with the Rotterdam sanitation department and made the soundwork possible:

I think the main reaction was enchantment—if I may be so immodest. The most common objects were transformed in people's eyes . . . All this happened in 10 very short and busy days. All of this work has a long history in the roots of modern Western art— from Futurist Machine dances, to early Russian Art, to German Dada, to Stravinsky and Fernand Léger— only I did it off the canvas in real life, not "realistic" but real—that's the advance. It takes very enlightened people like you and the Sanitation officials both here in New York City and in Rotterdam to make that possible. It is art of a different order of magnitude, because it involves real work systems being extended right into a cultural manifestation, self-consciously so. This is not clearly understood at this point in time.

2   See page 91 for the song's lyrics.

Follow the Leader

Snake

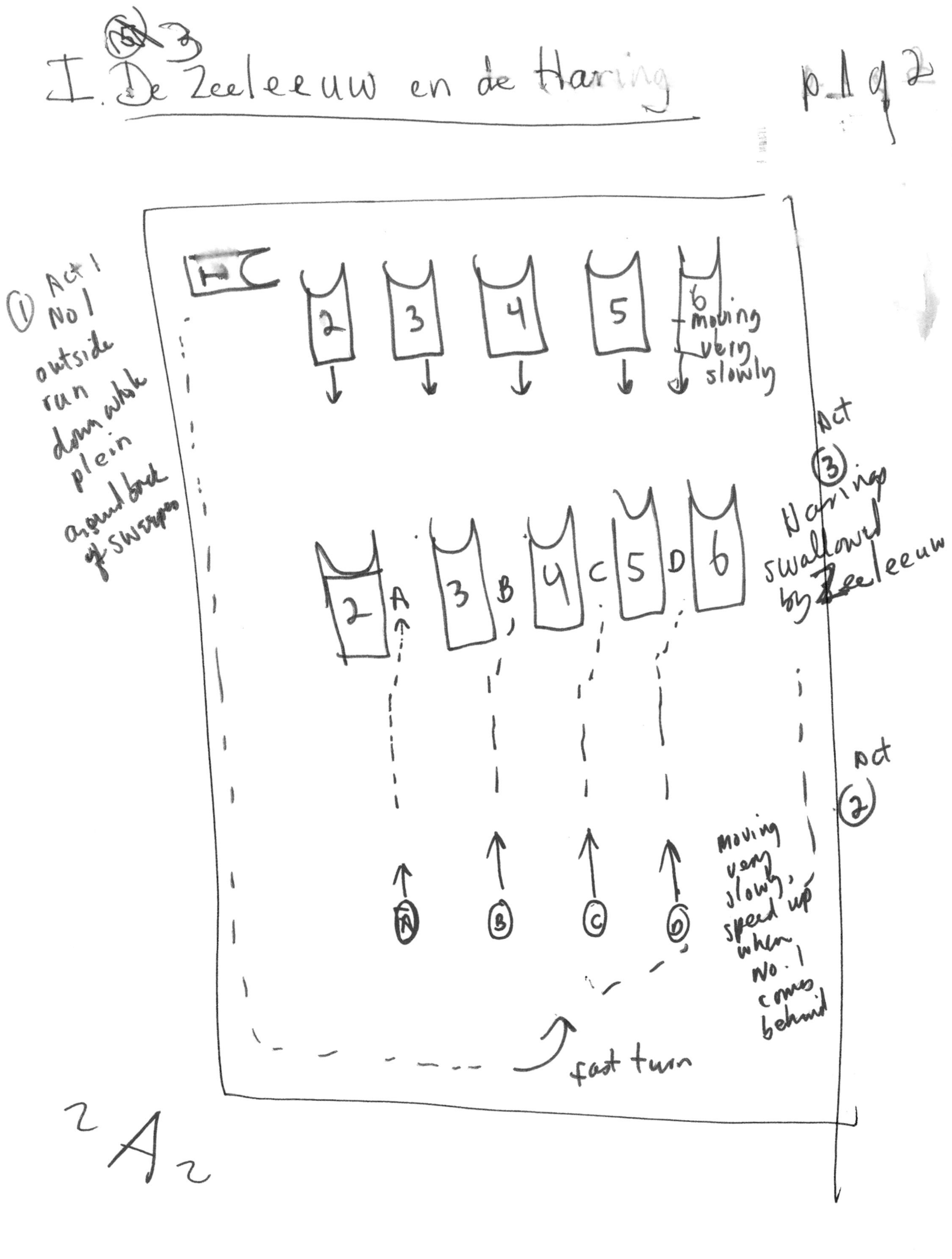

I. De Zeeleeuw en de Haring

p.1 q2

① Act 1
No 1
outside
run
down whole
plein
around back
of sweepers

HC

2   3   4   5   6 ┐ moving
                    │ very
                    └ slowly

2 A   3 B   4 C   5 D   6

A   B   C   D

③ Act
Harings
swallowed
by Zeeleeuw

② Act

moving
very
slowly,
speed up
when
No. 1
comes
behind

fast turn

² A₂

Drawing of choreography for *The Sea Lions Hunt the Herrings*

I. De Zeeleeuw en de Haring p. 2 q²

Step 4
A, B, C, D,
escape,
wobbling
with fright ε.
happiness
only 5 fun
No 7. Waiting
for them again

Repeat
whole
sequence
4 steps
2 opposite
direction

The Sea Lions Hunt the Herrings

Carousel

Carousel

Transition to *Hopper Cancan*

Hopper Cancan

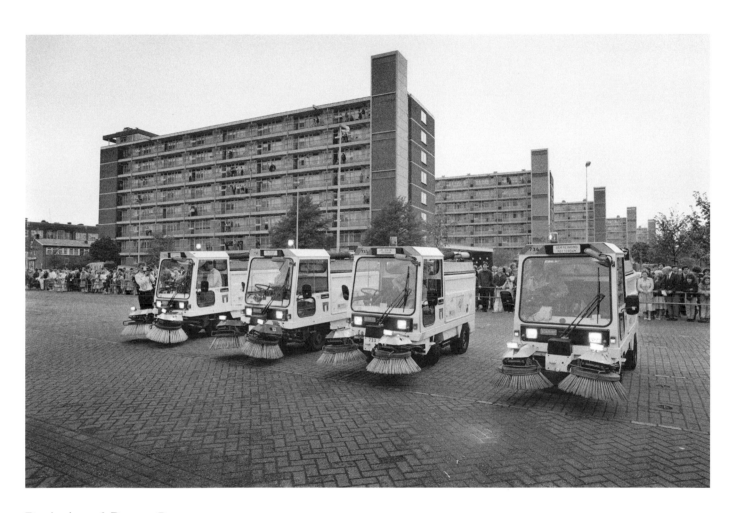

Beginning of *Broom Dance*

Ukeles conducting *Broom Dance*

Drivers joining community sing of "Laat het niet verder meer gaan" (Don't let it go on)

Laat het niet verder meer gaan

Song contributed by John Van Rijn
Don't let it go on

Vervuilde lucht	Polluted air
Vervuilde zee	" sea
Gif in de grond.	Toxin in th ground
Wat moet er mee?	What shall we do about it?
Heel even nog en de aarde is	One moment more & the earth is
geen plaats meer om te leven,	no more a place to live
leven, leven	to live to live

Refrein:

Laat het niet verder meer gaan	Don't let it go on
't gaat om ons eigen bestaan.	for its own existence
Laat 't niet verder meer gaan	
want de wereld is zo mooi.	when the world is so beautiful

De laatste kans	The last chance
De hoogste tijd	The highest time
Want straks dan zijn	If we go on
we alles kwijt	we lost everything
dan laten we de kinderen	If this happened
geen wereld om te leven	we don't leave the children
leven, leeeeven	a world to live, live, live

Laat het niet verder meer gaan
't gaat om ons eigen bestaan.
Laat 't niet verder meer gaan,
want de wereld is zo mooi.

3x Refrein

CREDITS AND DETAILS

VUILNISWAGENDANS (GARBAGE TRUCK DANCE)

DATE AND TIME
May 15, 1985
8:30–9:00 p.m.

LOCATION
Rotterdam, the Netherlands

SITE
The ballet took place at Visserijplein, a public square in West Rotterdam, eighty-six meters long and sixty-five meters wide. It was surrounded by residential apartment houses, small stores, and a community center.

The population of Rotterdam in 1985 was 1,035,000 people.

INVITING INSTITUTION, STAFF, AND OFFICIALS

Perfo 3 Festival:
Wink van Kempen, Director and Curator of *Vuilniswagendans*

LantarenVenster Cultural Center:
Fred van der Hilst, Director

City of Rotterdam, Department of Cleansing, Disinfection, Transport, and Workshop (ROTEB):
Hubert Kros, Director
J. C. Kalisvaart, First Deputy for Operations
Jahn van Rijn, Media and Education Director

Transnational technical support:
Paul Casowitz, Deputy Commissioner of Resource Recovery and Waste Disposal Planning, DSNY
Vito A. Turso, Deputy Commissioner of Public Information and Community Affairs, DSNY
Gloria Mills, Vice President, Ogden Martin, United States
Walter Martin, Ogden Martin, Munich and Rotterdam

MOVEMENTS

Movement I:	*Follow the Leader*
Movement II:	*Snake: Long Snake, Mini Snake, Crisscross*
Movement III:	*The Sea Lions Hunt the Herrings*
Movement IV:	*Ten Make Eight*
Movement V:	*Carousel*
Finale:	Part I: *Hopper Cancan* (garbage trucks)
	Part II: *Broom Dance/Borsteldans* (sweepers)
	Part III: *Bowing Dance* (all)
Community Sing:	"Laat het niet verder meer gaan" (Don't let it go on)
	(drivers and audience together)

SOUND WORK

Field recordings collected at the Ogden Martin Vuilnisbranding Institute, a barge-fed resource-recovery plant in Rotterdam that handled 999 tons of waste per day. The field recordings were collaged in a composition of industrial music that tracked garbage being transformed into electrical and steam energy and returned to the city. This work became the sound component, keyed to each part of the ballet, and was broadcast throughout Visserijplein, accompanying the ballet. It was recorded and collaged by Mierle Laderman Ukeles and Jahn van Rijn.

Other components of the project:

The ballet was followed by a parade of vehicles to the LantarenVenster Cultural Center, the festival's headquarters for a reception for all the drivers, their families, and officials.

A sculpture using materials from the ROTEB system was installed at the Perfo 3 festival exhibition at LantarenVenster Cultural Center, May 11–18, 1985.

VEHICLES AND DRIVERS

Drivers of six garbage collection trucks (*huisvuilwagen*):
John Beeris
Han Campen
Rijn van Eyck
Cor Hagesteijn
Hans van Herk
Ben Metaal

Drivers of four mechanical sweepers (*vaagmachine*):
Cor Blom
Bram Huijs
Ron Janssen
Theo van Kleef

DOCUMENTATION

Photography: Jannes Linders
Video footage (unedited): ROTEB

AUDIENCE

The audience consisted of 1,500 local residents around Visserijplein and beyond, including many children, attendees, and participants of the Perfo 3 festival, and various city officials. They sat and stood all along the perimeter of the square, several rows deep.

IV.

MOVIN' ON ALONG: BARGE AND TOWBOAT BALLET

INVITATION

In May 1991, guest curator Peter Boswell selected me to create an artwork for Pittsburgh's "Sculpture at the Point" exhibition for the 1992 Three Rivers Arts Festival. This three-week-long event was an important festival in the art world, and I wanted to be part of it.

THE SITE

When I first visited the festival's exhibition site at Point State Park, it blew me away; I had never seen an urban park so entwined with its geography. At the tip of the thirty-six-acre site and all along its edges, two big rivers—the Allegheny and the Monongahela—flow into each other to merge into a third, the Ohio River. It's an incredible visual watery confluence, right in downtown Pittsburgh.

Known as the "Forks of the Ohio," this swirl of rivers frames the city. Opposite the tip of the water-level park, along the shore across the rivers, everything suddenly rises. A long massive bluff with thick growth steeply rises 367 feet to Point of View Park on Mt. Washington. From the top of this park, there is a remarkably wide overlook view: one can see the whole urban landscape of rivers wrapping around the land below, with the dense high-rise city rising abruptly behind Point State Park.

PITTSBURGH

Apart from its natural proximity to the rivers, I was fascinated by Pittsburgh. Formerly one of the world's great river-based mining, manufacturing, and shipping centers, whose industrial base had largely disintegrated and evaporated, it was now reinventing itself. Its boom-and-bust history had such an impact on me personally that the city itself became a living character.

PROPOSALS

In the exhibition catalogue, Peter Boswell described what he called my proposed "grand vision": "She envisioned staging a multi-faceted ballet performed by some of the many vehicles that make Pittsburgh work: garbage trucks, police cars, fire trucks, coal barges, riverboats, and railroad trains and more."[1]

Enchanted by the layers of intermodal passageways over and around this flowing site, I especially wanted to coordinate the movement of trains—both those crossing the high bridges over the rivers and also those at water level traveling along the rivers' edges—in relation to the movements of barges on the rivers. I was inspired by the substantial barge traffic—the enormous and deep barges carrying coal and steel scrap and the colossal scale of the clusters of barges tied up along the shore opposite Point State Park.

No one on the festival staff, it turned out, had the energy to attempt to add intermodal train, barge, and municipal vehicle layers in the short time frame for planning the festival. The intermodal elements were dropped.

Mostly, I wanted to reveal these converging rivers as a still-functioning work site and to focus on the continuance of movement of work materials on the rivers. Bringing back the use of the classic, emblematic Pittsburgh materials—steel and glass but used in a new way—could show that the city, though changing, still retained the resonance of the "great old industrial days." By prying the materials away from the older, collapsed manufacturing culture, I could perhaps show how you can lose an industry, but through invention and productive work, still keep "movin' on along." A dance with steel, aluminum, and glass on all three rivers would reveal these materials anew; only

1   Quote from catalogue of the "Sculpture at the Point" exhibition, Three Rivers Arts Festival, Pittsburgh, 1992.

this time, these materials would be mined not from the earth but from the flow of recycling.

Back in New York City, I sent my ideas to the director of the festival, Jeanne Pearlman, and her festival staff, who became ingenious participants in local and regional research for recycled materials, towboats, barges, and facilities that could load tons of material onto barges. This was not a simple operation since barges filled with recyclables hadn't ever danced in this town.

I also wanted to honor the old-time steel workers who had worked in mills around Pittsburgh all their lives. The quality of the steel produced here had always been linked to the quality work of this highly skilled labor force. Yet after the industry largely tanked, the skies went dark, no longer lit up day and night by gigantic fiery furnaces powered by the workers' endless toil. Many companies went bankrupt and abandoned their workers, many of whom had chronic steel-related diseases and injuries. They were left high and dry with no health insurance and were mad as hell. Pearlman had introduced me to members of the Steelworkers Organization of Active Retirees (SOAR), who were leading the organizational effort to get the federal government to restore their health insurance. I invited these members to participate in the artwork and to join me in a public action as part of the ballet. They enthusiastically accepted.

Together with the festival staff, we settled on two simultaneous acts for the ballet. The first would be created on the rivers with towboats and barges filled with shaped recyclables, and the second would be choreographed together with the members of SOAR facing the towboats and barges along the shore at the tip of Point State Park.

PREPARATION FOR ACT I

I wanted to show new ways to present recyclable materials' use value and circulation by situating them on barges. We needed to finalize agreements to borrow materials and rent or get loans of barges. Beyond this we needed to secure cooperation from local handlers that do not usually work with recycled glass, bales of steel, or aluminum—but rather sand and gravel—to use their facilities to load the recyclables onto barges. The infrastructure to do this simply did not exist, nor did a system for designing and installing specific shapes in situ on barges. Solving these gaps required many leaps of imagination and practice to work across different government agencies and ma-

rine and materials industries. Ad hoc solutions for the ballet were invented collaboratively among all these groups, working along with the intrepid festival staff. This turned out to be one of the most creative aspects of the artwork.

I created two shapes for two of the barges: a sixty-ton recycled-glass mound in the shape of a diamond to signify value, and a ziggurat construction of eighty bales of flattened recycled steel and aluminum cans as a symbol of structures of elemental power. The glass diamond was achieved by creating a diamond-shaped base that I designed out of heavy timbers nailed onto the surface of a deck barge; then, at the sand and gravel depot, glass was poured from a great height until it accumulated to become a rough diamond— a glistening landscape. Besides being in the ballet, this first barge would be tied up along the shore of the park as a stationary sculpture for the entire three-week duration of the festival. The second barge, a hollow sand one, was filled up to its surface with soil, then covered with a blue tarp, so that the metal bales could be stacked all along its length then stacked incrementally until they became a long floating ziggurat. A third hollow barge, bigger and deeper, would be filled with huge hunks and columns of scrap steel.

This project was exciting yet nerve-racking up until the day of the performance. An oil spill the week before led to a coast guard warning that the rivers might need to be closed and the whole ballet canceled (which didn't happen). The final loading of the metal bales was completed only late the night before the ballet; at the last moment the provider for the scrap-steel barge was switched; and the insurance company introduced last-minute negotiations for the barges and materials. Only on the day of the ballet itself did everything get worked out. Whew!

PREPARATION FOR CHOREOGRAPHING THE BARGES ON THE RIVERS

James Guttman, head of Mon River Towing, a major towboat company in Pittsburgh, had tentatively agreed to provide towboats (called push boats in Pittsburgh) and barges for the ballet. Before Guttman would give his final approval, he stipulated that I needed to meet with Captain Charles Lowe to convince him that I could handle this choreography project using *his* push boats on *his* rivers. Guttman cautioned me that Lowe, a great expert on the rivers, was very territorial about who could get near the barges and who should be allowed on the rivers.

I approached this meeting with great trepidation. The day before, I went for a walk along the Allegheny River next to the tip of Point State Park to view the loaded red deck barge that had been brought up from the Mississippi River especially for my ballet. I arrived just as its deckhands were tying it up to the shore. Its green recycled-glass diamond was sparkling in the sun. The stakes for me were extremely high at this point: What if the captain said no the next day? Desperate to be able to say something meaningful to the captain at our meeting the next morning, I asked these deckhands, who weren't from the area and whom I'd never met before, "What is the hardest, trickiest, most dangerous thing you've ever done with your barge and push boats?" Their immediate, unhesitating answer: "Flop a barge." I had never heard this expression before and so they explained it to me.[2]

The next morning, I boarded the captain's push boat and walked back toward the kitchen where he was sitting at a table, waiting for me, looking at me quite coldly. He gestured that I should sit down across from him. I sat, faced him, and said, "Can you flop a barge?"

Bang! A small smile wandered across his face, almost melting it. "Of course." he said. I must have crossed some line or passed some test, because we got down to work immediately. I told him about other work ballets I had done, including *Marrying the Barges*. He told me about the uniqueness and the dangers of these three rivers, and how if a barge got away from the push boat and hit the columns of a bridge, the bridge could collapse and cause many fatalities.

Lowe said that Mon River Towing would provide three barges. The two push boats they would provide were called the *Express* and the *Explorer*. We worked out the following plan: He would be captain of the *Express*, which would push two barges. One would be the 135-foot-long deck barge that I saw the day before with its huge sixty-ton recycled-glass diamond. The second barge would hold the ziggurat of bales of flattened steel and aluminum cans. His son, Donald Lowe, would be the captain of the *Explorer*. It would push the third deep and long barge filled with hunks of recycled steel girders and other miscellaneous steel material that would come from a remaining active steel mill in the region. I asked if the coast guard could clear all three rivers during the ballet. He said he would try to get their participation.

We began to play out possible barge movements, using little rectangles cut from playing cards, pushing them around with our fingers. In this simple way, we worked out the choreography.

PREPARATION FOR ACT II WITH SOAR

During my research, I met with the members of SOAR at their offices and we went to work immediately. Wanting to build the choreography directly out of their work patterns and experience, I asked them to describe how they worked in the steel factories. They explained that the work environment was so noisy that you could hardly hear anyone speak. Steel was very heavy; the pieces were huge, often fiery hot and still molten. Communication with others on the floor and with crane operators moving high overhead was all physical and gestural, made with hand and arm movements. You had to pay attention to these gestures from others or you could get injured or killed. We developed a movement vocabulary that used these very same gestures they used on the work floor: *Take it up* (raise arm and point finger up), *Bring it down* (lower arm and point finger down), *Scrap it* (a chop-chop cutting gesture meaning "Remove this piece; not good"), *Take it away, over here* (swing arms toward self), and *Take it away, over there* (swing arms away from self).

We also choreographed a secondary group of movements where the retired workers held placards as if at a demonstration. On one side was their demand "National Health Insurance Now!" But for the blank side of the placards, we created a list of short poetic demands that they wrote out in big letters. These demands were for a kind of spiritual recycling of very active retirees. They insisted on literally presenting another side of themselves beyond their dire need for health insurance in order to be seen also as holistic individuals and not just aggressive demonstrators.

The sequence for manipulating the placards was worked out: "Hold up the 'Health Insurance' side. Then rotate the sign to our 'Special Message.' Lift the message up and down. Wave the sign overhead from side to side four times. Then turn the signs into a 'shovel' and make a shovel-scooping movement four times. Repeat."

The messages they drew on the backs of the placards were:

RECYCLE GLASS!
RECYCLE STEEL!
RECYCLE HOPE!
RECYCLE KNOW-HOW!
RECYCLE EXPERIENCE!
RECYCLE WISDOM!
RECYCLE DREAMS!

2   This maneuver can also be called "flip" or "top" a barge.

THE BALLET

ACT I: AT THE CONFLUENCE OF THE THREE RIVERS ON JUNE 21, 1992

The coast guard cleared the three rivers for two hours. The following is a description of the movements of the ballet based on my drawn diagrams. The quotations that follow are from a telephone conversation that I had in 2013 with Captain Charles Lowe, ninety years old, who still recalled the ballet from twenty-one years ago with great emotion.

CRISSCROSS

The two push boats came from opposite directions: *Express* came down Monongahela River (the Mon) pushing two linked barges to the West End Bridge, turned around, and faced the audience on the Point. *Explorer* came from the other direction down Allegheny River to the Point pushing the longest barge. The two boats met at the Point and crossed each other. *Explorer* then went up the Mon to the Fort Pitt Bridge, turned around, and came back to the Point.

FLOP A BARGE
AN EXTREMELY DRAMATIC MANEUVER

The *Express* flopped a barge to the barge on the left: moving one barge from one side to the other of another stationary barge in midstream, working with the current by "knocking the steel wires and ratchets loose, yet lengthening the lines that tie them together yet keeping them in check for safety," manipulating the barges against each other with the boats moving backward and forward. Then *Express* "unflopped" it.

The flop maneuver in the wide-open waters at the confluence of rivers looked magical and went off smooth as silk.

It was so mysterious that I asked Guttman to amplify Captain Lowe's short description and to comment on the drama and what I sensed was the danger in this move, and to clarify unflopping the barge. He explained: "The process of flopping a barge serves the purpose of placing a barge in a group of barges (a 'tow' of barges) so that the 'tow' is uniform in its width. The towboat never is unattached from the 'tow' and uses a combination of river current and a series of coming forward and backing (reverse) propulsion maneuvers in conjunction with precise manipulation of a barge line or rope which is controlled by the deck crew."

He continued: "The drama is that the barge that is being maneuvered appears to be somewhat inanimate because the captain and the deckhands are on the towboat. In reality each barge and its cargo weigh over 2,000 tons and once the idle barge starts moving its inertia makes it a formidable force. With river current behind it, the barge would soon reach the speed of the current if it got loose from the boat. So to move the barge from one side of the tow to the other by merely using a 60' line or rope is quite a feat which saves a lot of time because the alternative is to tie off the other barges and then go pick up the idle barge. And there are limited options as to where they would have been able to tie off the other barges."

The danger: "In the event that there is strong current, the idle barge that is to be picked up becomes a threat when it starts to swing around the tow. If a collision occurs with the other barges in tow, all of the lines and wires that keep the barges tied together could break under the sudden stress and the barges could break free from the boat and float away with the current until they can be retrieved. This is not a good situation in a river because there are many obstacles such as docks and bridge piers that must be avoided due to the narrow channel. As a matter of fact the term that is used when a barge hits an immovable object is called an allision. Not a term I like to use."[3]

And finally I asked, what about when the *Express* "unflopped" it? Guttman explained: "When Captain Lowe unflopped the barge he actually reversed the maneuver to show how a barge can be delivered to a dock when its position in the tow is on the opposite side from the dock. This again saves a lot of time and line handling if the barge can be delivered without having to tie off the tow for the purpose of delivering just one barge."

The push boats then tied up the three barges at the Mon River Landing across the river next to a group of coal barges. The barges remained there throughout the rest of the ballet. The remaining movements were done just with two push boats.

TOWBOAT DUET

Captain Lowe continued his description: *Express* went up the Mon and *Explorer* went up the Allegheny, then each came down the rivers and maneuvered around to face each other: "Face to face, head to head, head to boat. We did this with no lines, no ropes. We knew how to move our rudders to be able to do this without ropes. Then we kissed, kissed up. Put heads face up together, worked the rudders. Without ropes. Then we reversed engines."

At the signal of a whistle, *Explorer* came down to the Point and did a *donut*—a 360-degree turn-around while standing still in the river—then both did a *double donut* one way, clockwise, and a *double donut* counterclockwise the other way. "We locked boats head on, pushed each other, worked our rudders, made circles! Face to face. Like a flower in the middle of the three rivers, we made a flower form in the wakes spread out in the water." Then both made a 180-degree arc, a *half donut*, facing the Point toward the audience. Both headed down the Mon into the Ohio, reversed engines and backed up the Allegheny to the Duquesne Bridge and came forward, up the Mon, back up the Allegheny, to do the Snake. This final movement was done together, side by side: "*Snake, snake*, slithering together with only thirty, forty, fifty feet between us. A very tight, tough move."

As the ballet was ending, both boats stopped and did a "riverman's salute," one long blast followed by two short blasts of the horns. At that point, taking over the coast guard's loudspeaker, Captain Lowe announced that he was dedicating this ballet to his late brother Captain Donald R. Lowe, "a legend on these rivers for forty-five years," who had very recently passed away and was known as the other great push boat captain in Pittsburgh. Captain Charles Lowe, with his whole family standing with him on the push boat, was bursting with pride. Then the two-boat snake "slithered up the Mon" until it was gone.

ACT II: SIMULTANEOUS CHOREOGRAPHY WITH RETIRED STEEL WORKERS ON THE SHORE

Fifty retirees gathered at the tip of Point State Park and performed their movements, working together, at the same time as Act I's movements of push boats and barges were unfolding out on the rivers. Alternating between the group dance of their series of steel-mill floor gestures and raising their placards, they acted out the sequence of waving and scooping movements we had designed. Most importantly, they loudly chanted their poetic demands for spiritual recycling. They were in their sixties, seventies, and eighties, bursting with energy! It was amazing to be around them. The weather was awful, cold and rainy. It didn't put a crimp in the dancers' style at all.

I handed each retired steelworker my statement before we began the ballet. Here are some excerpts:

Thank you for your personal participation in this public artwork.

I wanted to create a work that expresses a desire to celebrate: value in work experience and know-how and value in materials beyond first use. These are precious treasures and should never be wasted. We cannot afford to waste wisdom and dedication and materials.

I could not create something like this without your participation. It is you who makes an artist's idea into something that is real and beautiful for all Pittsburgh.

I thank you from my heart.

Happy Barge and Towboat Ballet.

3   James Guttman, e-mail correspondence with the author, February 4, 2014.

Mierle Laderman Ukeles with supervisor, planning loading operation before ballet

Steel and aluminum bales being loaded onto the barge

Creating the sixty-ton glass diamond on the deck barge

Beginning of the ballet on the Monongahela River looking down from Point of View Park

Beginning of the ballet, push boats picking up barges

Ballet with Point State Park in the background

Flop a Barge

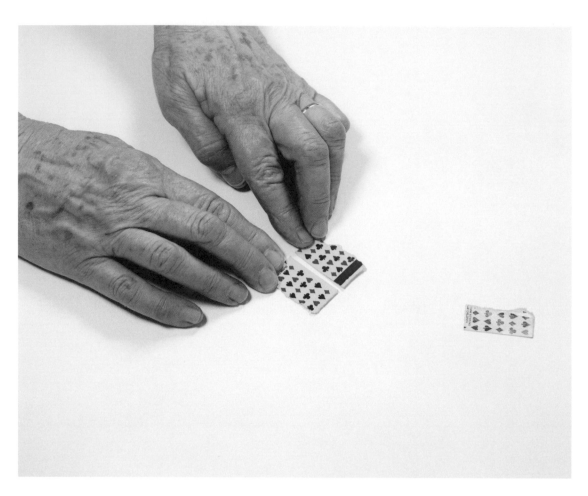

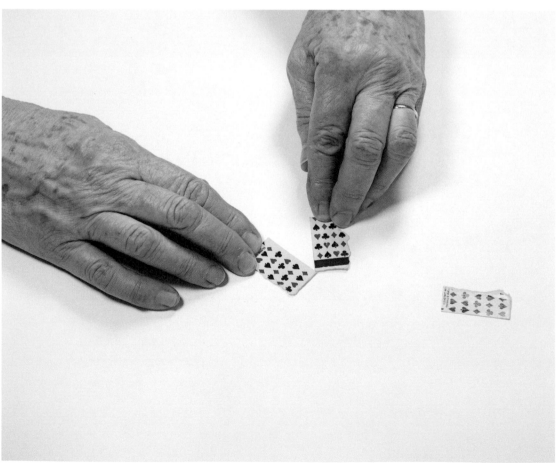

Mierle Laderman Ukeles choreographing *Flop a Barge*

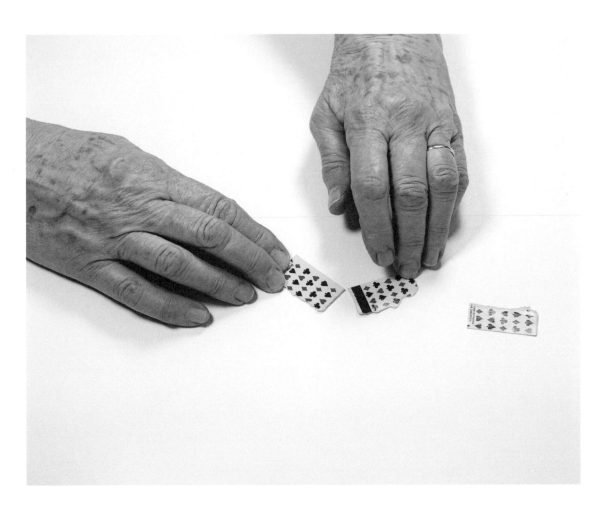

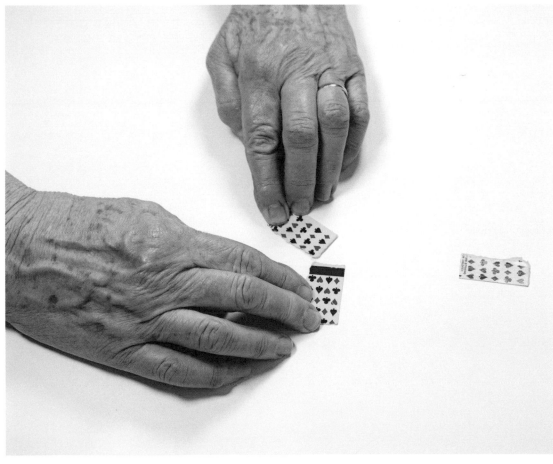

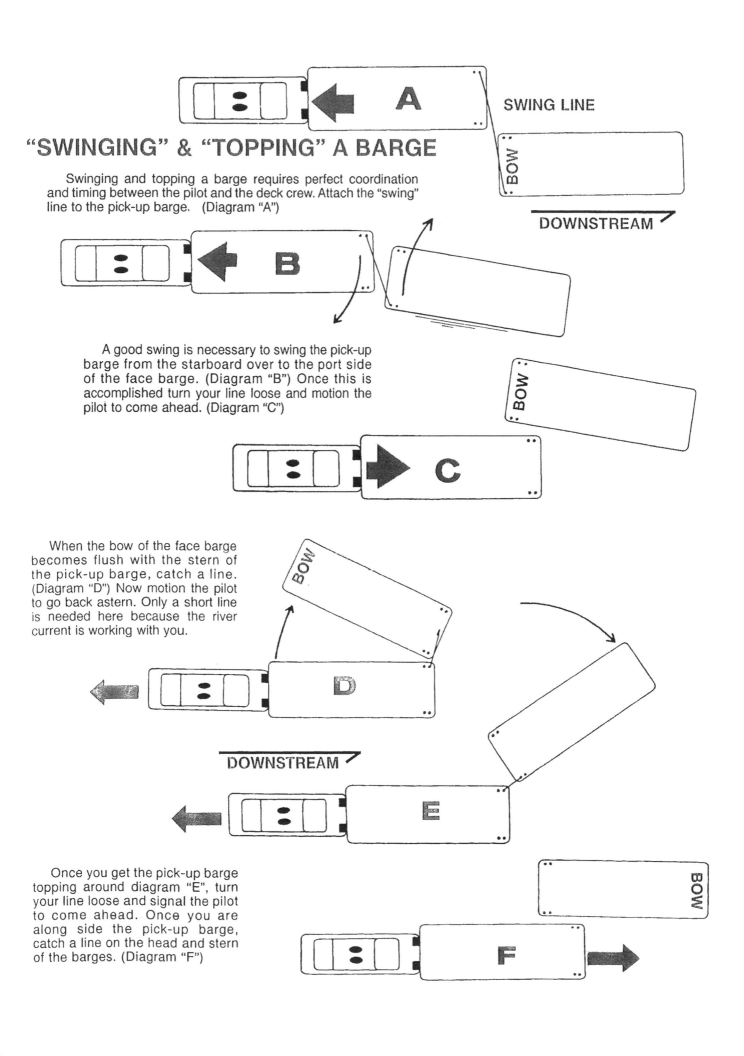

"SWINGING" & "TOPPING" A BARGE

Swinging and topping a barge requires perfect coordination and timing between the pilot and the deck crew. Attach the "swing" line to the pick-up barge. (Diagram "A")

SWING LINE

BOW

DOWNSTREAM

A

B

A good swing is necessary to swing the pick-up barge from the starboard over to the port side of the face barge. (Diagram "B") Once this is accomplished turn your line loose and motion the pilot to come ahead. (Diagram "C")

BOW

C

When the bow of the face barge becomes flush with the stern of the pick-up barge, catch a line. (Diagram "D") Now motion the pilot to go back astern. Only a short line is needed here because the river current is working with you.

BOW

D

DOWNSTREAM

E

Once you get the pick-up barge topping around diagram "E", turn your line loose and signal the pilot to come ahead. Once you are along side the pick-up barge, catch a line on the head and stern of the barges. (Diagram "F")

BOW

F

Tying up the barges at the Mon River Landing next to a group of coal barges

Towboat duet: *Double Donut*

Glass-diamond barge and steel and aluminum-cans barge tied up to coal barges

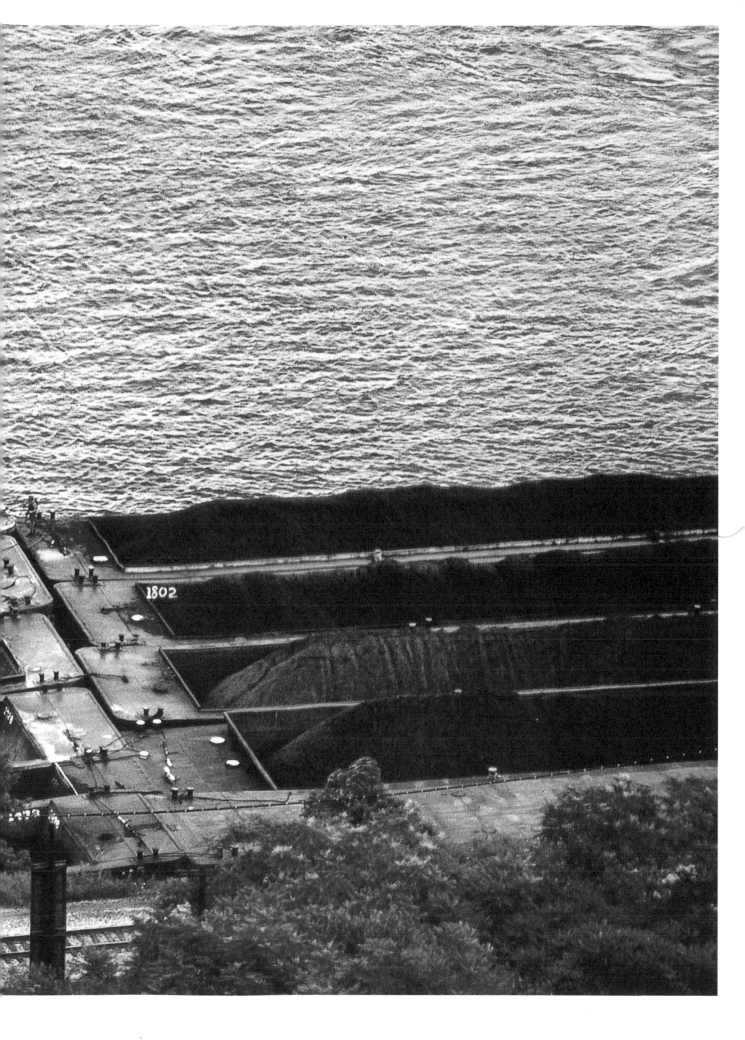

Choreography with fifty members of the Steelworkers Organization of Active Retirees (SOAR) at the shoreline of Point State Park

CREDITS AND DETAILS

MOVIN' ON ALONG: BARGE AND TOWBOAT BALLET

DATE AND TIME
June 21, 1992
12:00–1:00 p.m.:   Boats and barges gather
1:45 p.m.:   Coast guard clears the waterways
2:00–3:00 p.m.:   Ballet
3:10 p.m.:   All normal traffic resumes

LOCATION

Pittsburgh, Pennsylvania, United States

SITE

On the Allegheny and Monongahela Rivers with towboats and barges as they meet at the tip of
the Point State Park and then flow together into the Ohio River, and on shore with retired steelworkers at
the tip of the thirty-six-acre Point State Park.

The population of Pittsburgh in 1992 was approximately 370,000.

INVITING INSTITUTION, STAFF, AND OFFICIALS

Three Rivers Arts Festival:
Jeanne Pearlman, Executive Director
Peter Boswell, Festival Guest Curator and Associate Curator, Walker Art Center
Phil Harris, Project Assistant
Peter Boucher, Main Project Volunteer

US Coast Guard:
Lt. Commander David Eley
Chief Anthony Urban

Steelworkers Organization of Active Retirees (SOAR):
Marie Malagreca, Staff Coordinator
Jane Becker
Babe Dijosio
George Edwards
Anselmo Fernandez

Allegheny County Sheriff's Department:
Sheriff Coon
Lt. Rizzo, Boat Captain
Dick Rush, Boat Captain

MOVEMENTS

ACT I: Ballet with two towboats and three barges with recyclables with the following movements.

TOWBOATS AND BARGES
Crisscross
Flop a Barge: An Extremely Dramatic Maneuver

TOWBOAT DUET
Donut
Double Donut
Half Donut Arc
Snake
Riverman's Salute

ACT II: Simultaneous choreography with fifty retired steel workers on shore with three movements.

AUDIENCE

Along the edge of the rivers at the base of Point State Park.

BOATS, BARGES, CAPTAINS, AND CREW

Two towboats, *M/V Express* and *M/V Explorer*, each 65 feet long and 26 feet wide, were provided by James Guttman, president of Mon River Towing.

Captains:
Charles Lowe, *M/V Express*
Donald Lowe, *M/V Explorer*

Crew:
Bob Deems
Melvin Lowe
Mike Mathers
Robert Matznelli
Jim Simmons
Brian Watson
Evelyn F. Lowe, assistant

Barge 1: Glass-diamond barge, 135 feet long and 26 feet wide:
A deck barge with sixty tons of recycled crushed glass in a diamond shape 135 feet long and 26 feet wide, formed by pouring glass into a twelve-inch-high, diamond-shaped timber crib enclosure that captured the poured glass and established the diamond shape, constructed on the deck. This barge was tied up on the shore of the Point State Park and exhibited as a stationary sculpture throughout the duration of the festival.

Barge 2: Steel and aluminum-cans barge, 135 feet long and 26 feet wide:
A hollow sand barge, filled up to the surface with sand, on which a ziggurat-shaped construction was stacked of eighty bales of flattened steel and aluminum cans. The ziggurat was 98 feet long, 10 feet wide, and 6 feet high.

Barge 3: *MRT 104*, 195 feet long, 35 feet wide, and 12 feet deep:
This open hopper barge was filled with large pieces of recycled structural steel and other miscellaneous steel material, all estimated to weigh 1,500 tons.

Sources of barges and recycled materials:
Davison Sand and Gravel, Steve Jacobs
Dravo Basic Materials Inc., Jim Diecks
Barge Maintenance Inc., Richard Jackson
City of Pittsburgh, Department of Public Safety, Robert McCaughan
City of Pittsburgh, Recycling Division, Mary Beth Rizzuto
Commonwealth of Pennsylvania, Department of Environmental Resources
PA Glass Recycling Program, Douglas Gibboney
ASSAD Iron and Metals Inc., Jim Snyder
Owens Illinois Glass, Patty Hauser, Cheryl Laughlin, Bill Slater
Dlubak Glass, Dave Dlubak
Tube City IMS
ISRI Keystone Iron and Metal, Mary Lynn Thompson
Franklin Township Recycling Center, John Novaleski
SCRI, Jeff Landford
Alcoa Recycling, Russel Blackburn
Ohio River Towing, Midland Enterprises, David Gladwell
Weirton Steel Corporation, Herb Elish, John Turner, Charles Cronin
Azcon Corporation, Dave Ellis
US Steel Group, Susan M. Kapusta

DOCUMENTATION

Photography:
Kurt Weber

Video footage (unedited):
Rex Nordheimer, Videographer, directing ten cameras around the site

Sound:
Phil Harris

V.

RE-SPECT FOR GIVORS

INTRODUCTION

Givors is the smallest city in which I ever made a work of public art. The population of this ancient town along the Rhône River near Lyon is about nineteen thousand people. In the 1990s, the Communist town was suffering. Ever since France built the Autoroute A47 in Givors in 1968–70, an express highway that literally jumps over Givors, fewer people visit; they pass right over the town. Many residents have left and there is high unemployment. To counter this, the city of Givors created a plan to redevelop the Route Nationale 86 (RN 86), the original main road through town, and to turn its adjacent accumulation of old buildings, warehouses, and garages into a new central axis.

The Institut pour l'art et la ville, a Givors arts organization, added a cultural dimension to this plan in 1980 in order to interrogate the meaning of such towns caught by great urban changes. Thinking that a series of site-specific works by international artists might "show that art is involved in new domains and developing a new strategy of regenerating itself within the social body,"[1] they devised an experimental art program, "RN 86: L'art, la ville, la route." They selected curators to commission six contemporary artists in 1993 to create "interventions" accompanied by an international seminar. Tom Finkelpearl, the American curator, selected me in December 1992 and I accepted.

After an exploratory trip in June 1993, I sent several proposals to work with city workers, their vehicles, and barges on the river, and to use recycled glass. Jacky Vieux, the codirector, along with the project coordinator and my translator Amanda Crabtree, supported these proposals intensively, pursuing them with officials throughout the city. By July, the mayor had given them official backing for me to work directly with city departments.

1   Institut pour l'art et la ville, letter invitation to the author, January 29, 1993.

FRANÇOIS

I returned in early September. I had asked to meet with the city workers, and the organizers set it up. I presented a formal slide lecture of works I had done with service workers over many years in different cities and countries, so they could see how interested I was in their work, and that this kind of urban work was not only necessary but universal. I think most of the city's workers were in that big room—a benefit of working in a small town. I stressed that I would like to create a work with them, that I would not tell them what to do, but wanted to create something together. I told them that I had not worked in a Communist town before and assumed that in their Marxist labor culture, there would be great respect shown to blue-collar service workers. I asked, "Is this true? Do you feel your work is honored?"

They answered with great vehemence: "Nah! People say that we are goof-offs, that we're lazy and don't really earn all the money that we are paid. We are invisible!" These were the same statements I had heard for two decades from maintenance workers inside and outside of municipal governments. I was shocked and very disappointed.

Then at the back of this large room, a deep voice boomed out: "My name is François. If we work with you, do something with you, make something with you, will that get us respect?" He said it in such a hard, surly, and aggressive way, that it scared me. He put me on the line, and from that one person, the piece was initiated. I felt as if he was saying, "I'm stuck with reality; do you really have anything to offer or are you just weaving a fantasy?"

But I also felt that this was my chance. As long as someone was asking, then a door could be opened. I responded: "I don't know. If all these years of Marxist culture didn't give you respect, I don't know. But let's try!" I was so blown away by his challenge that I immediately named the piece—still uncreated—*Re-Spect* for *Givors*. This title has a double meaning: a work that demanded respect for the workers, and, just as important, *re-spect* from the Latin root *spectare*, to see again, to see anew: to see both those whose work makes Givors possible as a living city and, through them, a way to see the city itself anew. I knew that François would be watching me, to see if I was as serious as he was. From then on, I knew we had a beginning.

RESEARCH, CONCEPT, PREPARATION

What made a small town like Givors so rich to work in is that there was a strong cultural infrastructure in place that was as progressive and sophisticated as many cultural agencies in far bigger cities. My project coordinator and translator, Amanda Crabtree, was a first-rate art professional from the first moment I met her through to the end of the project. Jacky Vieux had also been Givors's minister of culture for many years, and thus had huge name recognition and had built up trust throughout the town and within the city government. Since Vieux was utterly supportive of what I wanted to do, doors opened up for me. Several other city officials asked me, "Do you want anything else?" after I had requested as much as I thought I could ever get. This had never happened to me anywhere else. When I went to see the head of the Givors fire department to invite his workers to create one of the movements of the ballet with me along the quai, I talked quite fast, as I usually did when I got a meeting with the head of a department elsewhere, knowing that such people were very busy and usually had very little time (or patience) to deal with an artist who was asking for their things.

"Would you like colored foam coming out of the fire hoses, Madame?" the head of the fire department volunteered. "What?" I couldn't believe my ears. "You're an artist. Color. We can give you colored foam and water. And what color would you like?" We settled on red foam and blue water. I was amazed.

I wanted to make a public ritual that enacted the continuing necessity of town services no matter what new redevelopment might occur. Old municipal organizational structures are key shapers of a city's infrastructure that will continue even as the city morphs into the future—the sanitation department equals cleanliness, health, and the most sustainable flow of materials into and out of the city; parks equals nature's ecological systems embedded as part of the city; fire equals safety and trust—all in the hands of human workers. These needs will always remain critical, and the workers will always need to be honored.

Further, this ritual could not stay only on RN 86, as the organizers originally intended. Any notion of a future city needed to link up the land and the water. Rivers are the life element of the town; Givors had a magnificent river. The river used to be the path for work, transportation, communication, connection—just like RN 86 had been. Both were paths that could still feed each other. I wanted to draw a new view, in three dimensions, to bring them together, to increase a flow from one to another.

EXPANDING "WHO IS GIVORS?"

Givors still had names to mark places that reflected its Communist past, such as Quai Julius et Ethel Rosenberg, Allée Ho Chi Minh, Avenue Lénine. I asked to be taken to these places. Several are in Les Vernes, a cluster of public-housing projects on the furthest edge of town. Who lived there? Mostly people from North African countries and Turkey who had immigrated to France by the prospect of jobs. Now, many of these people were caught both in the economic downturn and a stigma where, despite the fact that many were third-generation French citizens, they were still referred to openly and shamelessly by others as *les étrangers* (strangers, foreigners). I was struck when I was told: "The kids from this outlying area in this housing project have *never* been to the center of town."

Many of the older kids rode bikes up and down the low-rising hills upon which the projects are built. But they stayed there, very isolated. Many told me how trapped they felt. After visiting homes in the housing projects and meeting with residents, youth organizers, and teachers, I decided to include the kids in my Givors project. I had been discussing creating a parade with many city vehicles, right through the center of town, all along RN 86. I invited these kids to be in the parade right along with the trucks.

INDUSTRY AND RECYCLING:
PREPARATION FOR THE BALLET

Many former industries had packed up and left town. The most successful remaining industry was VMC, a large glass-recycling plant, continuing an industry active since the 1749 establishment of the Verrerie Royale (Royal Glass Works). On site visits, I discovered high mounds of crushed recyclable cobalt-blue glass. I fell in love with the crushed cobalt-blue glass mounds. I said that I needed 100 tons of this material for the ballet.

I proposed making a blue glass diamond,[2] the sign of value, to be hidden on a pontoon deck barge between two other barges as it floated down the Rhône, and revealed as a surprise for the audience at the conclusion of the ballet. It would be lit at the base by strong theatrical lights, so that it would appear radiant in the dark river. The proposal was accepted, but making it happen was not simple. No infrastructure to do this existed at the site. Alternative processes had to be created and unusual permissions received. Everything accomplished crossed boundaries.

THE ARTWORK IN TWO PARTS:
A PARADE ON ROUTE NATIONALE 86 AND
A BALLET ON THE RIVER

Part I was a parade of city vehicles and workers moving all the way through the center of town on RN 86, together with 100 kids from the Les Vernes housing projects. I ended up selecting over thirty vehicles from three different departments: sanitation, parks, and fire. On October 28, 1993, at 4:30 p.m., La Barquette, the city's fanfare marching band, led the procession and was followed by the municipal vehicles that presented themselves in a display of tremendous heft, in the presence of their fellow citizens, their families, and many international guests who had arrived for this project. There were so many workers who drove and serviced the trucks as a part of my project that the mayor dismissed all city workers that day for the parade and ballet!

As a counterweight, interspersed among the trucks, groups of the excited kids from the housing projects walked along flaunting grown-up-sized dirty work gloves from local industries, and waving them as symbols of power, to show that they could do real work in the city, and that they have agency.

Some also wore "identity costumes" they had made during months of workshops leading up to the ballet that expressed their being part of Givors. Their costumes were made of simple materials such as small boxes that were painted to look like urban buildings that fitted over their heads, becoming fierce-looking masks with holes for eyes and mouths. Each of these kids wore a big "G" placard or carried "Givors" signs as if they themselves had become the city. Some carried small floats with an environmental theme that they had constructed. My favorite was a group of girls who

had made a funeral bier transporting a laid out colorful tree that had been mercilessly cut down.

Other smaller groups of older kids on bikes did fancy turns that they had practiced for weeks, mimicking the big city trucks. These kids had finally been invited to the center of town. Their presence meant there was a place in Givors for everybody; they can see themselves and be seen anew, belonging as a part of all the citizens who could bring power to renew the city.

BALLET

The parade lasted about a half hour. Then the vehicles made a dramatic turn to the left, leaving RN 86, separating from the kids, and continued a few blocks, closely followed by many of the parade's spectators, along the street that honors the heroes of the Resistance, until they reached the edge of the Rhône. This was the site of Part II, a *ballet mécanique*, that took place on the five-hundred-meter-long Quai de la Navigation on the river's shore.

Since there is a history of flooding in the area, the non-river edge of the quai is the base of a massive long slanted seawall three meters high made of huge dark stones. It culminates on top in a park overlooking the river, called Promenade Maurice Thorez (a Communist Party hero). The regrouped audience, standing on the wide promenade behind the top of the seawall, had a panoramic view of the ballet that would take place down along the quai and out in the river.

In preparation, I had cooked up the choreographed moves together with each individual department, experimenting, inventing, then rehearsing directly on the quai, trying out different moves and ideas that culminated in three main movements on the quai and then another surprise in the river. Then, in rehearsals, we put it all together.

Amanda Crabtree told me that in between my three research and planning visits to Givors, the drivers of the various vehicles had developed a great competition—they brought their vehicles down to the quai after work to see how close to the river they could get during their moves. This was so extreme that during the actual performance I spent much of my time praying that no one would get so close to the edge of the river that they would flip over and fall in!

The town also offered some extra specialty vehicles: a bookmobile, a taxi, and two tall cherry

2   This diamond shape was to be similar in concept but larger than the one I made in Pittsburgh in 1992.

pickers. I grabbed this opportunity to use them to set the stage, and to have an intermezzo between the three major movements. The taxi did zany Charlie Chaplin zigzags chased by the lumbering bookmobile across the length of the quai from north to south and then exiting, only to reappear from the north again and again before each movement. The cherry pickers joined the sanitation-department movement and also offered a platform for taking aerial photographs.

MOVEMENT I: SANITATION

This movement was composed of eleven different kinds of sanitation trucks: big collection trucks, big and small mechanical sweepers, a snowplow, street-washing flusher trucks, dump trucks, and even a "Karchere," a custom-made odd-jobs truck they invented and cobbled together. The movement began as the trucks descended a slight slope under the Autoroute C47 bridge high overhead and entered very slowly and mysteriously from the north end of the quai. Gradually, one after the other, they filled the entire space of the quai in a long *serpent*, so close to each other as if connected by joints twisting and swerving all along the quai and back—all acting together in a flowing sinuous configuration that made these big clunky vehicles look surprisingly graceful. They each took a place and made tight circles right to the edge of the quai. Then each vehicle did a solo to highlight the individual worker. Some of the drivers of the flushers came up with a funny bit: they threaded a narrow hose through the top of a safety cone and when they ran water through it, it flopped around with unexpected wildness like a Tinguely kinetic sculpture. Everyone got wet. On one of the big orange collection trucks, we opened the side panels so the viewers could get a Duchampian view of the hydraulic sexual parts of the truck operating, as the mighty hopper rose up and down, up and down. The two cherry pickers, one thirteen meters and the other seventeen meters high, in position on the south end of the quai, began to slowly come to the same level and kiss! The thirteen-meter cherry picker descended and exited with all the other vehicles at the south end of the quai. The seventeen-meter one—whose platform supported photographers—stayed.

MOVEMENT II: PARKS

Since the eight parks trucks were smaller vehicles, the scale of the ballet became more intimate and even nimble. A little tractor, a forklift, mowers, a grass picker-upper, and a seeder—some of the vehicles even showed up unexpectedly filled with arrays of flowers, a surprise for me. Entering in single file from the north and moving south, all together, they made a *serpent* and returned in a *crisscross* all along the quai. Each vehicle then did a solo, some to the left and some to the right. One, riding right along the edge of the quai, kept tipping the fenced-in open back of his vehicle from side to side to such a degree that it made you hold your breath. Each exited after his solo. The largest and most dramatic vehicle, the B90 seeder, carried a high pyramid that the workers had constructed of chrysanthemums and other autumn plants. It crossed the whole space, then departed. All vehicles exited from the south end of the quai.

MOVEMENT III: FIRE

The quai was now empty, the sun low on the horizon. Darkness descended throughout this movement. An eerie ambulance-siren sound was heard while the fire trucks were still "offstage." It was a great relief to be able to hear these sounds as sound and not as an alarm that something dangerous is happening.

They approached. The vehicles turned on their lights. There were two boxy medium-sized fire engines, a fire ambulance, and a giant twenty-four-meter ladder truck. They entered from the north, descended the little slope, and performed the following moves on the quai: simple *serpent* toward the south, then *double serpent* returning toward the north; *crisscross* toward the south, then *spider* (*la araignée*), a kind of flying wedge, with sirens turned on, upon returning toward the north; then a *spiral, zigzag, spiral* toward the south to take up positions and pause. The ambulance had a solo: lit up from inside, the drivers came out of the truck with a stretcher, performed a mock life-saving maneuver, and returned inside the ambulance. Then it crossed the quai toward the north and exited, while the other vehicles stayed in place throughout the finale.

The fire sequence concluded with a special series of moves at the edge of the quai and over the river. (A foam-making *mousse* truck and a water-jet machine had been placed out of sight on ramps just below the middle of the quai before the ballet, ready to provide foam and water to the firefighters.) The huge ladder truck, positioned in the middle of the quai, faced the river. Its two drivers extended its ladder twenty meters up and outward, cantilevered over the water. Four fire fighters climbed the twenty-four-meter-high ladder in the darkness, carrying a huge hose that sent an arc of clear water out over the river like a very high fountain, as if they were climbing to the full moon already shining brightly overhead.

To the north of the ladder, a firefighter in a high-tech silver heat suit stood on the edge of the quai facing the river, holding a fire hose out over it. The water-jet machine fed blue water to his hose, which sent it out in an arc over and into the river like another fountain. On the other side of the ladder, to the south, another firefighter in a high-tech silver heat suit, standing on the edge of the quai, faced the river holding a fire hose outward. The foam machine fed red water to his hose, which sent an arc of red foam over and into the river like a foamy fountain. Water to water—these ritualistic gestures coming from the firefighters, so purely aesthetic with no rhyme or reason other than that it looked so beautiful, gave the piece a layer of poetry beyond words—a notion of return, the return of power and energy back to us and the river.

A SURPRISE FINALE ON THE RIVER

All three truck movements were performed on the quai next to the river. On the river, an informal gathering of various small crafts appeared, each with some relation to the city, to increase the surprise of what was to come on the river. Before the first movement, a fast fire motorboat, named *D'Artagnan*, zoomed clear across the river and disappeared. Two small boats with cheery men in old-time costumes who belonged to a long-lasting association of lifesavers rowed alongside the quai throughout the ballet. All this time, during the three truck movements, a stream of barges and boats had quietly passed by on the river—as they do in regular life. A trio of lashed-together barges appeared from the north under the huge, high overhead bridge of the Autoroute C47. Together, they passed by the audience, moving with the fast current, and continued beyond the south end of the quai. At first, they looked no different from other barge traffic moving by on the river. Then, something changed. They stopped just before they reached the Pont Suspendu de Chasse, which was quite a bit beyond the quai. They made a wide slow turn all the way around, still moving together, and began a puzzling return trip northward. Then these three lashed-together vessels, still from a distance, shifted slowly and began to approach the audience: two narrow covered barges and, in the middle, a wide pontoon deck barge. All of a sudden,

the two narrow barges dropped the ropes binding them to the deck barge, pulled sharply away and did a squiggly-wiggly tango dance against the current, then moved aside. They were like midwives whose work had been completed. The deck barge shot forward—newly born on the water. It carried a mysterious cobalt-blue glass mound rising to a point, suddenly lit-up and visible from quite a distance. A push boat appeared and pushed the blue-diamond barge slowly toward the audience until it kissed the quai. The two narrow barges zigzagged away single file to the other side of the river.

This sight was delivered by a group of people who were very calm, competent, and at ease in the water environment. It was dangerous and required a level of skill by trying to do certain patterns despite the risk of the current's hard and fast flow. They pushed themselves to the limit.

The blue-diamond barge nestled up to the edge of the quai, so that the mass of the glowing blueness became fully apparent as the night grew darker and darker—a 100-ton diamond gift to the audience. I was standing high up on the seawall, along with an enraptured audience, accompanied by Aïcha, a young girl from the housing projects waving her big dirty work glove. The ballet was over.

After awhile, the push boat moved the diamond pontoon a bit south on the river to the Maison du Rhône, where it was tied to the dock. It was a breathtaking sight. Many people went down to the river's edge all night long to stand there and swoon in the glow of this diamond. A lady said to me, "You've returned the river to us tonight." The next day, the diamond was returned to the recycling yard, delivered into the fire to be reborn as cobalt-blue dishes, cups, and saucers.

TWO DAYS LATER

I stayed over the weekend in the one small hotel in Givors, wiped out. I heard a knock at the door on Saturday afternoon. It was two hotel maids. One of them introduced herself as the wife of François, the worker who had asked me at the very beginning if working with me would get them respect. "You did good! A very good job!" she said.

AFTERWORD

Jacky Vieux sent follow-up comments to me at the New York City Department of Sanitation via fax on November 11, 1993:

Dear Mierle,

I hope you and Tom got back o.k.?

It is now time to go over what happened here: even before RE-SPECT *emerged, I was interested in the project in its refusal of models, the desire to link art and life.*

I lived this intense moment like a ritual.

Since, I have thought of Walter Benjamin, his concern with the opposition between society and community, the "cocooning" effect on private life provoked by the exaggerated developments of technology. In spite of this, how can we keep the narrative?

Benjamin speaks of similarities between holidays ("feast days") and works of art as a meeting with a former life. He envisages the artistic symbol as a means of revealing a new object of experience, a reality we had been unable to name.

On October 28, you made a new language be spoken in Givors, a language which existed already in men and all things.

Thank you for this and for many unforgettable moments.

On January 3, 1994, I sent the following fax to the organizers in Givors:

My dear friends,

I miss you and Givors.
I will never forget you and the magic we made together.
The River—called out to, in wholeness, by the town.
The children's shining eyes.
The workers watching each other.
The grace and fearsomeness of the machines.
Kids watching workers.
Minds playing, visible in machines.
And, forever, the blue diamond.

It is actually unbelievable to me what we did. This only happens rarely in one's lifetime.

So you are so precious to me. I thank you.
Can you think of a way to thank so many many who made this?

Entrance of vehicles to begin the parade on Route Nationale 86

Parade turning left toward the river

Mierle Laderman Ukeles, Jacky Vieux, and kids from the housing estates marching in the parade

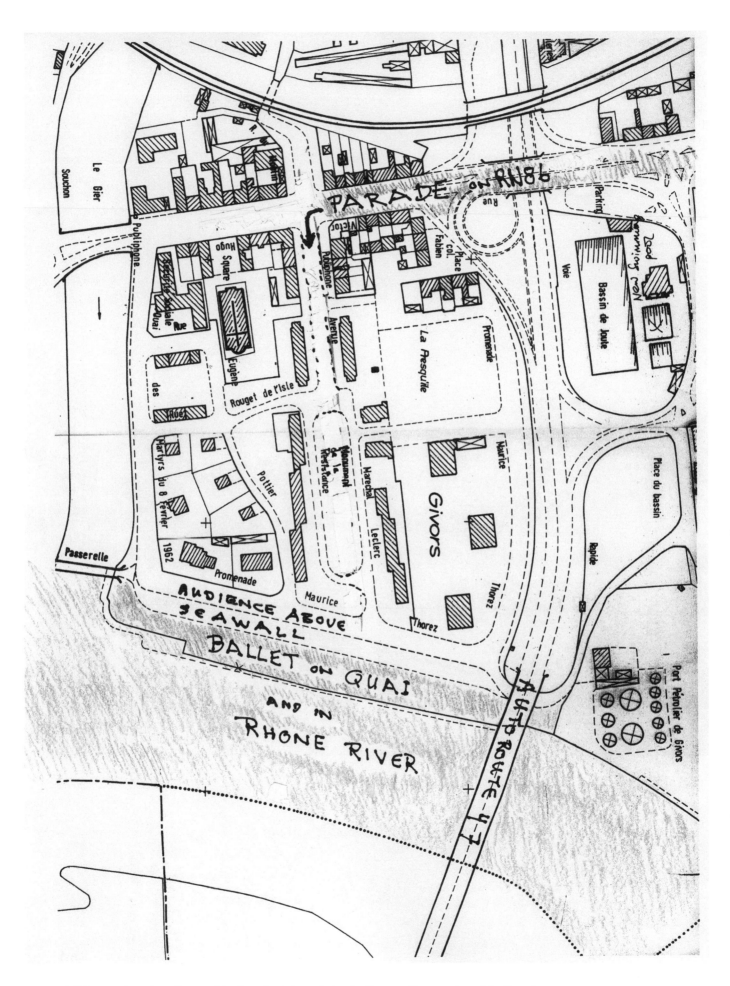

Map of Givors showing Route Nationale 86 and the ballet on the quai and in the river

Parade participants

Movement I: Entrance of sanitation department vehicles onto the quai and the audience on top of the seawall

Serpent

Sanitation department vehicles: solos

Movement II: Parks department vehicles

Parks department vehicles with pyramid of plants

Movement III: Fire department vehicles and ladder truck

Firefighter delivering colored water to the river

Movement IV: Three barges on the river

The surprise liberation of the *Blue Diamond*

Blue Diamond approaching the audience

CREDITS AND DETAILS

RE-SPECT FOR GIVORS

DATE AND TIME
October 28, 1993
4:30 p.m.:   Parade
5:00 p.m.:   Ballet on the Quai de la Navigation and in the Rhône River
6:00 p.m.:   Reception at the Maison du Rhône and viewing of the diamond

LOCATION

Givors, France

SITE

The parade proceeded through the middle of town along Route Nationale 86 and the ballet took place along the Quai de la Navigation and on the Rhône River.

The population of Givors in 1993 was approximately 19,000.

INVITING INSTITUTION, STAFF, AND OFFICIALS

L'institut pour l'art et la ville (Institute for Art and the City):
Alain Charre and Jacky Vieux, Codirectors
Tom Finkelpearl, United States Consultant and Curator
Amanda Crabtree, Translator and Project Administrator

In collaboration with:
city of Givors
Givors Fire Department
VMC Glassworks Rive-de-Gier
Rhône Navigation Department, Lyon

Supported by:
Ministry of Culture/Visual Arts Department, Paris
DRAC Rhône-Alpes/Regional Arts Bureau, Lyon
Ministry of Equipment, Paris
Head Office of Architecture and Urbanism, Paris

With the participation of:
Sports and Cultural Association of Vernes
Primary schools of the City of Givors
Association Bibliobus Intercollectivités
Chambre Nationale de la Batellerie Artisanale
Association Bi-Cross
Association des Sauveteurs

PARTS AND MOVEMENTS

PART I: A PARADE ON ROUTE NATIONALE 86
La Barquette: city marching band
Sanitation Department
Parks Department
One hundred schoolchildren
Bookmobile
Fire Department, Part 1
Teenagers on BMX bicycles
Fire Department, Part 2
Taxi

PART II: A BALLET ON THE RIVER
Movement I: Sanitation Department
Movement II: Parks Department
Movement III: Fire Department
Movement IV: Surprise Finale on the River
(Intermezzi: between all three movements: bibliobus, taxi, cherry pickers)

VEHICLES, BOATS, BARGES, AND PARTICIPANTS

La Barquette: city marching band

Sanitation Department (*La voirie*):
One white garbage collection truck (*la benne à ordures blanche*)
Two orange garbage collection trucks (*les bennes à ordures oranges*)
One small mechanical sweeper (*la petite balayeuse*)
One large mechanical sweeper (*la grande balayeuse*)
One unique custom-made odd-jobs truck (*la karchere menagerie*)
One snowplow and salt spreader (*le chasse-neige/le camion de sel*)
Four flushers: backhoe (*la tractopelle*), dump truck (*le camion benne*), Manitou forklift (*le chariot élévateur*),
leaf blower (*un souffleur de feuilles*)
Two cherry pickers (*deux nacelles*)

Parks Department (*Service des Espaces Verts*):
One Mam truck, one Aebi truck, one Holder tractor, one little forklift with different attachments, one Yno truck,
two J9 mowers, Renault B90 Turbo truck with pyramid of plants and chrysanthemum flowers

One hundred schoolchildren

Bookmobile (*Le Bibliobus*)

Fire Department (Part 1) (*Les Pompiers*):
One fire truck (*le camion de pompiers 1*), two fire trucks (*les camions de pompiers 2*)

Four teenagers on BMX bicycles:
Their teacher described the sequence: "The cyclists repeated the following sequence of moves:
bi-cross doing a sequence of wheeling, 360 degrees to 180 degrees, bunny-up, up to the small bridge of
the road, single file on the small bridge, and after the bridge repeating the sequence."

Fire Department (Part 2) (*Les pompiers*):
One ladder truck (*le camion pompier échelle*)

Taxi

On the river:
Two canal barges (*les péniches*), one pontoon barge (*le ponton*), one pusher boat (*le pousseur*)

Blue Diamond: A mound of crushed recyclable cobalt-blue glass, three meters high at the peak and weighing 100 tons; held by a diamond-shaped wooden crib of timbers fixed to the deck of the pontoon barge. It measured 11 meters long by 5 meters high with theatrical lights around the base of the glass.

Ceremonial rowing boats, some manned by the centuries-old Lifesaving Society of Givors (*Association des Sauveteurs*)

Fire department speedboat (*D'Artagnan*)

AUDIENCE

The audience, estimated at several thousand people, stood on the Promenade Maurice Thorez in the park overlooking the river above the quai.

VI.

SNOW WORKERS' BALLET 2003

INTRODUCTION

In 2002, I was invited by curator Tom Finkelpearl to create a site-specific artwork for the 2nd Echigo-Tsumari Triennial. The region called Echigo-Tsumari in the Japanese Alps has among the highest annual snowfalls in the world, averaging around four meters of snow every year. That is higher than the ground floor of most buildings! It is a farming and blue-collar region with towns, houses, and stores, not an alpine resort. But in the last few years, large numbers of young people have left, choosing an urban experience over the ancient, often backbreaking tradition of rice farming as well as the isolating winters. Many schools in the region were empty; the population was aging. In an effort to combat this depopulation, the regional government came up with an ambitious multiyear effort to lure people back to this extraordinarily beautiful region through a series of triennials of contemporary art, commissioning local and international artists to travel to the region to create site-specific art. They also commissioned architects to design several permanent cultural centers and local museums.

The belief that a series of cultural works and events can bring new thinking, new interest, and new resources to highly challenged cities or regions is similar to the situation that led to the site commissions in Givors in 1993. I always wonder if people are putting too much faith in the generative powers of art.

When I learned about the site and the out-of-this-world average annual snowfall, I became very intrigued. As the Artist-in-Residence in the New York City Department of Sanitation since 1977, I know that snow is serious. When there is a blizzard, there is nothing like it in terms of high emotion, determination, and even dread. It is war. They call snow work "blood money." So when I heard about the snowfall in Echigo-Tsumari, I wanted to meet their snow-truck drivers. It was obvious to me that it was these fearless drivers who made it possible for people to live here in the winter. Without them opening the way throughout the winter, no one could survive.

The triennial brought me on my very first trip to Japan in August 2002 to do research. I started in Tokyo where I met Fram Kitagawa, the conceptualizer and general director of the triennial and also head of Tokyo's Art Front Gallery, along with his sophisticated professional staff. They emphasized that they were all committed to creating a new appreciation of the challenged Echigo-Tsumari region, which included showing great respect to its inhabitants. Afterward I was taken on a long drive to Niigata Prefecture to travel around the Echigo-Tsumari region.

The region has multiple shades of green: bright green from the rice fields and the deepest green from the incredibly thick and abundant forests. The area's beauty, especially the geometry of the rice fields in relation to the curvy masses of the dense forests that run right down into the towns and villages, was breathtaking.

The terrain, in many places, is very hilly. I wondered how people were able to traverse these roads when they got icy and snow-packed. We came upon a municipal garage where several snow vehicles were lined up outside. I asked about them, and was told they are called rotaries. I had never seen anything like them, anywhere. It's Japan: even the snow trucks are magnificently designed! They have huge red spiral cutting blades that would slice through the snow, then suck it up into flexible, rotatable "shooters" so that the driver could direct the snow in arcing plumes, off the road and out of the way. Lined up, they were already a ballet! I was more eager than ever to meet those snow-truck drivers.

A meeting was arranged. Entering their garage, we took off our shoes and went upstairs. Everyone was sitting on mats around a big pot of boiling water, so we could all have tea and talk. If sanitation workers in New York City would see me in this comforting setting, they would faint. None of the workers spoke any

English, so we talked to each other entirely through translators. I told them a bit about my earlier works with city service workers in other cities and countries. Then, on a hunch, I said to them, "I bet in the winter, everybody loves you. Is that right?" Translation. Everyone in the room nodded yes. I continued, "I bet in the summer, everybody forgets all about you. Right?" Everyone immediately nodded yes. Vigorously. "Well, next summer, let's remind them. OK?" Enthusiastic agreement. I was in: we could create a ballet together. I met the boss, Mr. Kanetaka, a reserved polite man who was very much in charge. It was agreed that I would work directly with him. However, I insisted, and they agreed, that I could also work directly with the workers.

Upon my return home to New York, I found myself in an unusual dilemma: the entire rural landscape and most of the culture had been strange to me. I had never worked in such an environment before. Yet the work condition and the workers' situation were familiar; I felt I knew a lot about them both. I refused to make my work in New York that would then be shipped over and plunked into place. I wanted to create a site-specific work that could only be done there, with the local workers, about them, on their turf—even though we hardly knew each other. So, after my research trip, I took a chance to offer my own interpretation of the reality as I saw it. Here are a few excerpts from my concept sent to Fram Kitagawa on December 31, 2002:

Snow is the essence here.

When it becomes a big fat body that lies down over the whole place and blocks the way, suffocating passages and openings, it becomes terrifying. Yet, strangely, in its quiet heavy beauty, its abundance fertilizes the coming majestic rice fields and magnificent trees. The culture of this place springs out of the human response to its terrifying and awesome embrace.

The primary culture-makers of this place are those who work the snow. Opening the way, they wrestle the devil for us. Wonderful machines are their blazing armor. The endurance and shrewd courage of these snow workers keep this place alive. We are completely dependent upon them.

Yet in the summer we forget, and these heroes usually fade into the background. Yet it is also in the summer that there is enough easy weather to take a big breath, and then to take the time to honor them, to shower them with our love as they flex their muscles— purely—in front of our eyes.

Together, we can embrace the hard deal that Nature has doled out here and fight back with bravado. They must be the best drivers there are!

Together, they come up with movements that come out of the secrets of their great expertise in the winter. Only now, they perform these magical movements in the summer, in full view, with no battle, just pure energy and amazing beauty floating on ripples of reality-memories. Actually reality feeds pure fantasy.

After a series of proposals, we agreed that my project would have three components: first, a *ballet mécanique* in Tokamachi; second, a two-monitor video with one monitor showing the regular snow work, to be shot during the approaching winter, and the other monitor showing the ballet in the coming summer; and third, *Warm House*, site to be determined, an installation that would be a meeting place with tables and chairs for snow workers and visitors to get to know each other. *Warm House* would include the two videos, photographs from the ballet, and the drawings of the choreography, to be on view throughout the fifty-day duration of the triennial.

NEW YORK / JAPAN PLANNING AND NEGOTIATING FROM A GREAT DISTANCE

Between January and July 2003, right up until I arrived in Japan to create the work on July 9, many issues about the artwork were debated and negotiated via e-mail between me and the triennial staff coordinators for my artwork—Hiroko Seki at first, and then Yoji Tobita, who managed the project through to its completion.

The great distance was painful; depending on e-mail for basic communication was excruciating. In April I sent a revised proposal to try to clarify the essence of my concept: "I propose to consider the creation of the ballet—dreaming up the choreography together between the drivers and myself—as very much part of the artwork, so that the process of creation and the final creation is a continuing and much larger artwork." Now despite a general acceptance of this statement, or rather no one ever straight-out rejecting it, there were bureaucratic gaps, budget gaps, and probably significant cultural gaps. They wanted me to make three trips to choreograph the ballet months in advance and to tell the drivers what to do, so that when I would come to Japan in July, before the actual performance, everything would have been done. I refused. I insisted that we do everything together right before and up to the performance itself in July. They finally accepted this. They wanted me to work with the drivers after work, on break, with no days of rehearsal. I countered: "The drivers need time to get over thinking how weird this is and to allow their talents to come out. I cannot do this kind of work without their being able to have the freedom that comes with worktime... We need three full days." Finally, on June 23, I was able to get three full days where the drivers would be excused from work altogether. This was a big expense for them.

I wanted the trucks painted because they looked scruffy. Not possible. What's more, I needed a full-time translator, because ease of communication was critical to being able to trust each other enough to work together. I explained why I felt this was so necessary: "There is a safety factor so that if I say 'left' they do not turn 'right'. This could be a very dangerous artwork with people crashing and getting run over unless there is excellent and accurate communications with everyone!" I finally got a great translator from the region who stayed with me throughout. Everyone needed walkie-talkies. I wrote, "It is urgent that we communicate during the ballet." Hard, but they got them. Even the number of trucks I would have to work with wasn't settled until about two weeks before I arrived. And, as late as one week before I arrived, I was still asking that the following be explained to the drivers: "I am coming with NO preconception of what this will look like; I admire their skill tremendously and they know much much more about what their trucks can do than I ever will; that this is a chance to do something that they fantasized about and never had a chance to do—what they would like to do with their truck when officials were not looking; how much people count on them in the middle of the winter; that I want their everyday-looking trucks to appear to become MAGIC right in front of the audience—and are popped out of their normal habitual context." I ended up feeling that I got the best deal that the triennial was able to offer and I arrived in great spirits and hopefulness.

The site was terrific: a long rectangular field, one hundred fifty meters long and seventy-five meters wide, alongside the big broad Shinano River. Crossing over the top edge of the field was the Tsumari-Ohashi Bridge. The audience would be able to stand either on the bridge perpendicular to the river, overlooking the field (like in Givors), or down on the ground, level with the trucks, along the long front of the field, parallel to the river. A thicket of trees formed the bottom edge of the field opposite the bridge.

I had three full days for rehearsals. We began our work out in the field so I could see how these trucks operated. I had never seen a rotary operate before. There were six big rotaries with blazing red spiral cutters in front and one baby rotary for Mr. Kanetaka, the boss. Then there were three huge tire dozers with yellow, green, and red blades, one midsize green dozer, and one strange midsize yellow dozer with a butterfly blade. This blade had a vertical center pin that divided it into two winglike parts that were connected to the pin. That way, it could operate like a regular unitary blade, but also had the flexibility of waving both its two wings separately. These last two trucks were not as large as the big tire dozers. Then there was a long highway construction vehicle called the motor grader, which had huge wheels that could tilt sharply and quickly to the left and to the right while the truck was moving, with a narrow, very long rotating blade underneath in the middle. It looked like a praying mantis but with big eyes (lights) and was very fierce looking, stranger, and much longer than the other vehicles.

I had to work very fast, because I did not get any extra time for planning meetings and discussions with the drivers. We alternated between field and garage, coming back to the garage to talk through different possible moves.

After the first day and a half of rehearsals, I felt I was getting nowhere. The ballet was coming along okay, but it needed something special, unexpected. We had already worked on a special dance for the rotaries, and we needed something for the tire dozers, the other major group of snow vehicles. I stood in front of the group of drivers, who were seated all around the meeting room, waiting. I turned to face the blackboard to draw possible movements. I had my back to the workers, desperate and yelling at myself, "Come up with something!" I had been feeling bad for the two drivers of the midsize tire dozers, since these weren't like the other three huge powerful tire dozers, nor did they have the fabulous design of the big rotaries and their red spiral cutting blades and shooters or the darling cuteness of the baby rotary, and they weren't scary or weird like the motor grader. They were just ordinary farm machines, middling-size tire dozers. One would never pay them any attention as they drove by. I wanted to give them a special role, something that would make them stand out and be memorable despite their ordinariness. I recalled that in Japanese literature there is a great appetite for love stories, and in classic theater a tradition of high ritual performance where it's natural for men to play women's roles. Suddenly, my idea just showed up. I turned back around to the drivers and said, "Do you know the story of Romeo and Juliet? You know, the young lovers from families that hate each other, that are enemies?" Translation. Everyone nodded and my translator said, "Yes, they all know the story." So I replied, "How would you like to do the story of Romeo and Juliet with trucks?" They all nodded yes. I turned to the two drivers of the ordinary tire dozers and asked them, "Would you be Romeo and would you be Juliet?" Each said yes.

That night, on July 15, I e-mailed my husband Jack in New York: "Today was the first good day really I was so scared practically into paralysis but I pushed through it and the drivers are really amazing and terrific. I didn't know what the hell I was doing but I just made it up."

Walkie-talkies were given to each driver, Mr. Kanetaka, the project manager Yoji Tobita, and my translator Ayako Yoshino, as we would need to communicate across a very large area. I drew diagrams on a board and the drivers changed and corrected them. We returned to the field and tried out moves again. Each time they rehearsed, their high skill level enabled them to work closer and closer to each other, to make their moves sharper and more articulated. They were able to work almost touching each other. For such big machines, this was a sight to behold.

The weather was mild and easy to work in. I felt as if I was getting to know the drivers and they were getting to know me. At a certain point, I noticed one of the drivers wasn't there; he hadn't returned after a break. I went across the field to the river looking for him, and found him far down the steep banks of the river, at the edge of the water, bent over a shrine of river stones that he had made to enable his work to come out right. He was praying. Despite not having a language in common, I had felt that we had achieved great communion; nevertheless, I realized here that there were major gaps between our cultures.

Mr. Kanetaka directed on his walkie-talkie from inside the baby rotary. He also joined a few of the actions. He had a great style. I trusted him. It was coming together.

I completed a full set of drawings with Ayako on Friday. I drew diagrams of the moves and described them in English; Ayako wrote the descriptions in Japanese. The drawings looked like ancient Japanese scroll paintings with writing integrated into the drawing. She took them to be photocopied and distributed to each driver to keep in their truck cabs during the performance.

DAY OF THE PERFORMANCE

On Sunday morning, the day of the performance, there was to be a final rehearsal before the performance with the audience. The *Snow Workers' Ballet 2003* had been selected for the official tour schedule of the triennial, one of a small selection of the over 150 commissioned works to be visited by the large group of international visitors and curators who come to the triennial.

We woke up to what sounded like light hammering on the roof. I didn't know what it was, then it dawned on me: it was raining. There hadn't been a hint of rain all week—the weather had been good and mild. We went to the rehearsal early and asked Mr. Kanetaka if the ballet should be postponed. He smiled and said, not at all; we work in bad weather. Of course, whom did I think I was talking to? We proceeded with the final rehearsal.

It rained straight through the performance. The field was very muddy with deep tracks cut into the surface by the truck movements. The spirit among the drivers was so high that it didn't really matter.

MOVEMENT I: DEFINE THE BOUNDARIES OF THE STAGE

All the vehicles gathered outside the space. At a signal, they started beeping their horns. Then they entered in a single file, quite close together, and moved completely around the perimeter of the field. This gave the audience a chance to see the "dancers," a chance to perceive and feel the huge size of the "stage," and also—a big goal of mine—a way to perceive the larger context all around, the Shinano River, the hillside rising up along the other shore of the Shinano, the wide Tsumari-Ohashi Bridge, the big open sky arching above. These deep landscape spaces became framed between the moving trucks.

Then, the *snake*. This was a chance to populate the interior space of the field. All the vehicles were involved, one after the other in single file, gradually developing multiple narrow lanes as the move progressed, across the width of the field, turning at the edge of the river, then coming back to the front of the field. The drivers' skills were acute. They crossed at the midpoint of the field exactly at the same time as the vehicles in the next lanes. At the beginning of the movement, there was only one lane in use with the first vehicles, but as it developed, it swelled with more and more vehicles entering, moving through the lanes. At the midpoint of this move, they looked like one connected, breathing machine. It really was like a snake growing longer, twisting, puffing up, then expanding and contracting with great fluid power. Gradually, the snake contracted, diminishing in size just as it began.

MOVEMENT II: DANCE OF THE DOZERS: THE TRAGIC LOVE STORY OF ROMEO AND JULIET

In the version of *Romeo and Juliet* we worked out, the young lovers had already found each other and had fallen deeply in love. Their love was radiating, despite the hatred flowing between their two families. The three big tire dozers were the chorus. Their job was to protect the young lovers. The tire dozers did a power dance to show how protective they could be. The young lovers entered and faced each other in the middle of the vast field. The chorus was behind them and off to the side, guarding them. They approached each other and did a dance of ecstatic love. Nothing else mattered in the world.

This chorus of tire dozers—even though they were the biggest and strongest of all the trucks—were narcissistic goof-offs. They were supposed to protect the young lovers; yet, full of overweening pride, they neglected to pay attention.

The young lovers tenderly came closer to each other. They were thrilled with each other even though their families were enemies. They proclaimed their love, unafraid. In the dance the drivers created, the trucks faced each other. They raised their blades again and again, moving them closer and closer, within a hair's breadth of each other. The blades embraced. Actually this was a very dangerous move. If they executed it wrong and hit each other, they could have tipped each other over. But they did not. They came closer and closer together. I could hear people swooning, *Ooooooooh.* The hard trucks produced a highly sensuous softness. They echoed what the festival's sophisticated and well-known photographer, Anzai, had called out while shooting this scene during the rehearsal, suddenly naive: "This is soooo emotional!"

Ecstasy before doom. Again and again, they raised their blades to the sky, butterfly blades flung wide open, oblivious of anything else. Shockingly, the fickle dozer chorus abandoned the lovers and moved to show off in front of the audience overhead on the bridge. They were so busy playing like showgirls to the audience, raising and swaying their blades this way and that, they completely did not notice the lurking evil motor grader hiding under the bridge. He darted out behind their backs and, brazenly beeping his loud horn, he attacked. Dashing right between the couple, he sundered their embrace and destroyed them. Their courage evaporated; they left the field, blades dragging, totally defeated. The baby rotary was outraged and chased the giant motor grader all over the field in a fury. The motor grader, frightened, ran away. The baby rotary, his daring challenge coming too late, was left alone on the field. Tragedy unfolded.

To me, it is amazing how a range of genuine human emotions can rise up out of hard machines! But I see also that it was the snow workers' intense and courageous tenderness to express these feelings coupled with their great skill that determined what we saw.

MOVEMENT III: DANCE OF THE ROTARIES

The dance of the rotaries had three parts. First, the *zigzag*: the six big rotaries formed three tight couples so close they almost touched each other. Led by Mr. Kanetaka in his baby rotary, they did a huge *zigzag* movement across the entire space, starting from the southern front corner of the field near the audience, and then cut a diagonal across half of the field to its midpoint near the river, crisply turning to cut another diagonal across the other half of the field, coming back to the opposite northern front corner of the field. They moved so close to each other that it looked as if they were one connected yellow and red machine. Their crisp angular movement was the closest reference in this ballet to early twentieth-century Constructivist mechanical dance.

The second move, the *running spiral*, was like a game of tag. Lined up across the field, the first rotary made a spiraling, twisting turnabout that culminated in lightly touching the next rotary in line. Each of the six continued this action, which looked like a chain reaction of stopping, twirling, and setting off the next rotary, until the energy flowed through all of them across the field.

The third move was called the *snow shooters' dance.* All six big lumbering rotaries came right up to the path that divided them from the audience on the ground of the field. Mr. Kanetaka in his baby rotary joined the lineup, nestled in among the middle of the big guys in line, to face the audience. In winter, the shooters collect the snow sucked in and up by the big rotating and cutting spiral blade. The snow is then blown away from the vehicle and the road in beautiful arcs. Here, there was no snow to shoot. So we worked out a routine where the shooters, which started out lying in front of the driver's cabs, slowly rose up, turned this way and that in synchronized movement with each vehicle, and then twirled all the way around. It looked very friendly and countered the rather intimidating proximity of the big vehicles to the audience. Most people had never been so close to one of these vehicles, and here they were, facing them eye to eye. Then all the rotaries slightly rose up in place, on their "haunches," and spun their spiral blades full force. It was thrilling!

MOVEMENT IV: FINALE

All thirteen vehicles participated in two moves for the finale.

First, in *come to the audience and bow*, the tire dozers and motor grader joined the rotaries and lined up to face the audience on the ground. Together the vehicles turned away from the audience and headed across the field all the way to the river as if they were leaving. At the river they quickly reversed with their back-up beepers blaring. In the middle of the field, they turned very slowly, as if in a Noh dance, and came tiptoeing toward the audience. When all the vehicles had completed this slow turn, each was on its own, each driver deciding how to gesture to the audience, bowing, swaying, tilting and sliding blades, raising and lowering twirling spirals, shooters dipping and turning, flashing lights on and off, honking horns a lot, and generally making gestures signaling connection as they came right up to the audience, to the spectators' delight.

The second and final move was the *long diagonal*. From their positions at the end of the first move, where all the vehicles were lined up next to each other on the edge of the field, facing the audience, the first vehicle, nearest the southeast corner of the thicket end of the field, stayed still, while the rest began to very slowly move back. Each one successively stopped further and further back so that a sweeping diagonal of snow trucks was formed that spanned clear across the space. The last vehicle nearest the bridge at the northwest end of the field was furthest back from the audience, almost at the river. Then each driver got out of his truck, stood in front, and took a bow.

The performance was exceptional. Stunning. The local people who were used to seeing these vehicles make it possible for them to live in the area in the winter were amazed to see them transformed into mak-

ing something so different and beautiful, and to have the chance to be in such close touch with the drivers. These workers had made their brute machines appear so delicate and graceful that looking at this mysterious scene from a distance—snow machines swirling in a summer field beside the big river—they popped out of the prison of their winter cage and looked like magical beings dancing naturally in this majestic landscape.

Mierle Laderman Ukeles during rehearsal of *Dance of the Dozers: The Tragic Love Story of Romeo and Juliet*

Define the Boundaries of the Stage

Dance of the Dozers: The Tragic Love Story of Romeo and Juliet

Romeo and Juliet

Dance of the Rotaries: Zigzag

Finale: *Come to the Audience and Bow*

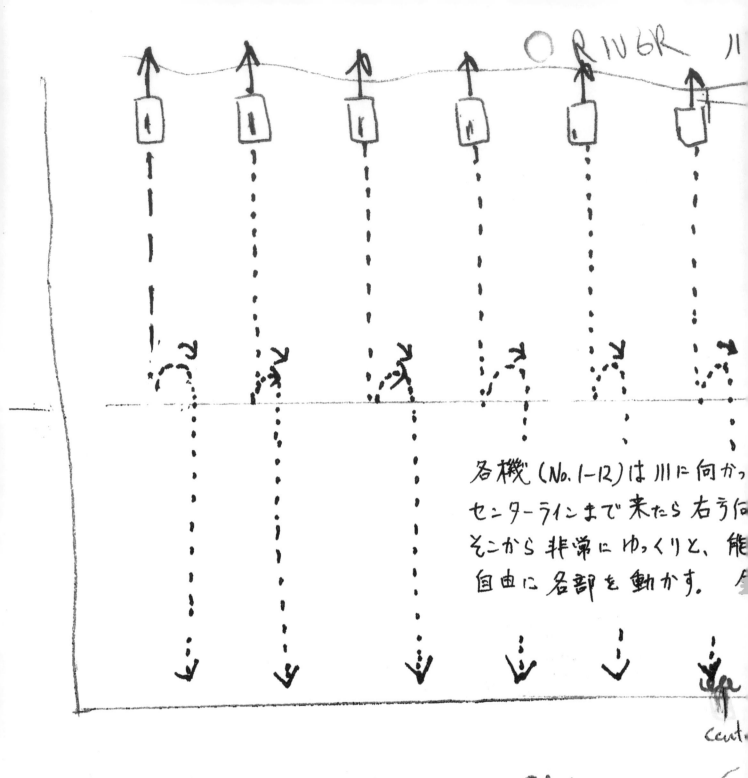

各機 (No. 1-12) は 川に 向か
センターラインまで 来たら 右う向
そこから 非常に ゆっくりと、能
自由に 各部を 動かす。

ORIVGR

cent

IV.1. FINALE
フィナーレ

EACH TRUCK (#
EACH BACKS U
MAKES A SEMICI
THEN, TOGETHER,
COMES TO AUDI
GESTURING DRIVE

Drawing of choreography for *Come to the Audience and Bow*

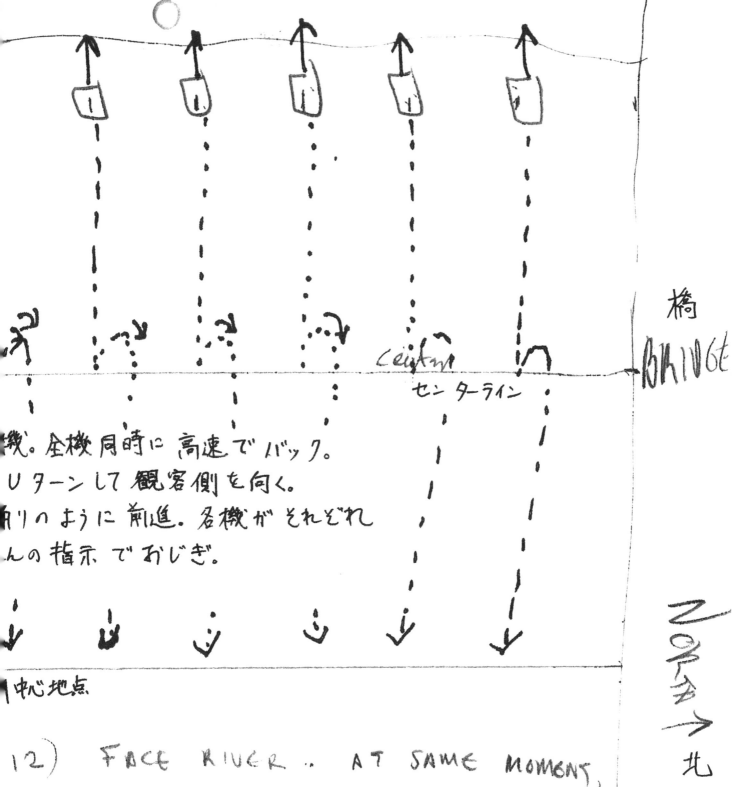

橋
BRIDGE

Center
センターライン

機。全機同時に高速でバック。
Uターンして観客側を向く。
踊りのように前進. 各機がそれぞれ
〜んの指示でおじぎ。

中心地点

NORTH →
北

12) FACE RIVER .. AT SAME MOMENT,

FAST TO CENTER LINE (East/WEST)

E TO RIGHT UNTIL EACH FACES AUDIENCE.

Y SLOWLY, LIKE A NOH DANCE, EACH

E - WITH WHATEVER PART OF TRUCK

NTS. BOW AS MR. KANETAKA DIRECTS.

The thirteen drivers of *Snow Workers' Ballet 2003*

CREDITS AND DETAILS

SNOW WORKERS' BALLET 2003

DATE AND TIME

July 21, 2003
11:00 a.m.–12:00 p.m.

July 25–September 7, 2003
Warm House video installation

LOCATION

Tokamachi, Niigata Prefecture, Japan

SITE

The ballet took place alongside the Shinano River on a field 150 meters long and 75 meters wide.
The installation *Warm House*, drawings, and photographic portraits of the drivers were shown at the Kinare
(Triennial Center).

Tokamachi had a population of 42,000 in 2003 and the most snowfall on Japan's main island of Honshu
among cities of its size and larger.

INVITING INSTITUTION, STAFF, AND OFFICIALS

Echigo-Tsumari Triennial 2003:
Fram Kitagawa, General Director
Toshio Kondo, International Artist Project Coordinator
Yoji Tobita, Project Manager of *Snow Workers' Ballet*
Yasunari Kumagai, Coordinator of International Artists
Hiroko Seki, Early Coordinator
Ayano Yamaguchi, Support Staff
Ayako Yoshino, Translator

MOVEMENTS

Movement I: *Define the Boundaries of the Stage* and *Snake*
Movement II: *Dance of the Dozers: The Tragic Love Story of Romeo and Juliet*
Movement III: *Dance of the Rotaries: Zigzag, Running Spiral*, and *Snow Shooters' Dance*
Movement IV: Finale: *Come to the Audience and Bow* and *Long Diagonal*

VEHICLES AND DRIVERS

Thirteen snow vehicles:
Three large tire dozers with red, green, and yellow blades
One medium tire dozer with green blade, "Juliet"
One medium tire dozer with yellow butterfly blade, "Romeo"
Six large rotaries

One baby rotary
One motor grader

Supervisor and conductor:
Tamotsu Kanetaka

Drivers of snow tire dozers:
Kunio Miyazawa, "Romeo," medium dozer with yellow butterfly blade
Kazuo Murayama, "Juliet," medium dozer with green blade
Akira Nishikata, large dozer with red blade
Yasunari Niwano, large dozer with yellow blade
Masashi Oshima, large dozer with green blade

Driver of the motor grader:
Haruyoshi Yanagi

Drivers of the rotaries:
Hideoshi Abe
Mitsugi Fukuzaki
Kazuyoshi Iizuka
Takashi Miyazawa
Yuichi Murayama
Hirohiko Nogami

DOCUMENTATION

Photography:
Shigeo Anzai

Video footage (unedited):
Masaki Ogawa

Televised footage:
Takahisa Araki

AUDIENCE

The audience, estimated at four hundred people, was in two locations: alongside the southeastern edge of the field on the same level as the vehicles, separated by a path and guard ropes, and on the Tsumari-Ohashi Bridge, over the northeastern edge of the field overlooking the river and the field.

VII.

SNOW WORKERS' BALLET 2012

INTRODUCTION

I loved making the *Snow Workers' Ballet 2003*, but when it was finished, I thought my connection to the triennial was completed.

On March 4, 2011, I was amazed to receive a letter from Fram Kitagawa, the general director of the Echigo-Tsumari Art Triennial. He wrote: "It's already eight years since you worked with us at Echigo-Tsumari Art Triennial. I still remember the impact of your work when I saw it . . . back in 2003. . . . I am always thinking that your project was one of the best works I saw in Echigo-Tsumari. I am dreaming of working with you again . . . in 2012."

I received this letter exactly one week before Japan's cascading disasters of the earthquake, tsunami, and Fukushima nuclear meltdown that resulted in 19,000 people dead or missing. Even though the Echigo-Tsumari region is separated by a mountain range from the tsunami and Fukushima, it too experienced a severe earthquake. Surely, I thought, the triennial would have to be canceled or at least postponed. I was wrong. In August 2011, I received another letter asking me to visit Japan for a research trip.

RESEARCH TRIP

I set aside my concerns about radiation, and made a four-day trip in November 2011, going to the region with Toshio Kondo from the triennial along with the videographer Takahisa Araki, who had produced a terrific segment of the *Snow Workers' Ballet 2003* for Japanese national television. We drove up to the region to make a plan and meet people from 2003 as well as new possible drivers.

Arriving in the city of Tokamachi, we gathered in the same familiar garage again to meet with old and new workers, with the workers sitting on mats around a big teapot steaming in the middle of the room. I was so happy to see several drivers and my wonderful translator from 2003. I hugged each of them, and probably embarrassed them. It was as if time had melted away. It turned out that the man who played Romeo in 2003 was still called Romeo by everyone in the garage!

I had never done a work ballet in the same place twice. It was both familiar and strange. Most of the drivers were new, as were the representatives from the city and the region who also attended. The triennial staff showed the drivers Araki's television program and the complete set of choreography drawings from 2003. I told them that the 2003 ballet was one of my best artworks. Explaining how we did it in 2003, I said, "Together we kind of make it up." The drivers from that time nodded in agreement. Then I continued talking to the new drivers, feeling strongly that this was a new Japan after the recent natural disasters and Fukushima. I said, "The subject of the human facing Nature, what Nature brings, is a very, very important subject all over the whole world. You make it possible for people to live here, even in the winter. No matter what happens, you will be there, and you will keep working to make a path for everybody. You are as strong as the Snow."

There was a new boss, Mitsugi Fukuzaki, one of the drivers from 2003. The previous boss, Mr. Kanetaka, with whom I had worked so well, had retired. I needed to show Mr. Fukuzaki that I recognized that he is the boss now, and that everyone needed this clear affirmation of my acceptance of him in his new role. I asked him to be the conductor of the ballet. He flashed a broad, brand new smile, and accepted. Everyone wanted us to do *Romeo and Juliet* again. But Romeo from 2003 had another job and was not available, nor was Juliet, who had retired. Since they were fabulous in 2003 I was worried whether we could find workers who would be as good for 2012. I reiterated my commitment that we would all create the ballet together. I felt that with new drivers, we were starting all over again.

We went to see the snow vehicles. They asked me to choose what I wanted, and I asked how many I could have. Thirteen at most, they said. I grabbed all thirteen immediately. There were new rotaries with two spirals: the same big vertical snow-cutting spiral as before, but on top, a thinner horizontal moveable rotary cutting blade called a "swing ogre." Being able to choose among all the vehicles I liked, I said, "This is like being in heaven." Araki agreed to go to the region during the hard winter months so we could get great "real" footage of snow.

It was a very productive trip. Soon after I got back to New York City, Kondo e-mailed that they would freshen up all the bulldozers' bucket blades with new paint—a big change from 2003, where they were quite grungy and workaday and my requests to paint them were refused. They asked, besides the traditional yellow, red, and green for the dozers, would I like special colors for Romeo and Juliet? I chose a royal purple for Romeo and a soft and seductive peach for Juliet, peach being an important color for fruit in much Japanese art.

In the winter, Araki would spend several days with the snow drivers shooting the snow work. This footage became one of the two-monitor videos shown the day after the first performance and throughout the triennial in my installation at the Kinare, now called the Satoyama Museum of Art, the main exhibition space of the triennial.

JAPAN, SUMMER 2012

We arrived in Japan on July 19. Three performances were scheduled: I would be present for the first performance in July, a second one would be in August, and the final one in September. Kondo and Yoji Tobita, whom I worked with in 2003, would direct these latter two works. Besides a day of meetings in July with public officials, I had three-and-a-half days of rehearsals with the drivers, plus a dress rehearsal early on the day of the performance.

With my new translator Azusa Ono, the officials, and the triennial staff, we first made a site visit to see the newly painted dozers, including Romeo and Juliet. As I had suspected from photographs of vehicles that had been sent to me earlier, Juliet was bigger with a much longer, larger blade, not of middling size and relatively delicate as before. Now she was a big girl! She was as big as Romeo! How would Romeo be able to embrace her? I was nervous.

We shifted our focus to the newly painted vehicles. It turned out that the vehicle painter, who was also one of the new drivers, used to be a detail painter for Toyota. His glossy bright colors on the bulldozer blades were simply gorgeous! Perfect. He had treated every truck as if it were a racecar. The edges of all the newly painted blades zinged! The paint was so ravishingly reflective that the blades became sculptural concave objects that captured, scooped up, and flipped over the panorama of landscape and sky inside their curved blades as they moved. He even painted the motor grader blade, tires, and hubcaps a shiny, wicked-looking black.

That afternoon when we met with the public officials at the site of the ballet, a nervous atmosphere pervaded. They gave me a new set of tougher restrictions that reflected the hard reality resulting from the traumas of the earthquakes and tsunami: the ballet would be canceled outright, even at the last moment, if the Shinano River, which bordered the site for the performance, rose above a certain height. No audience would be allowed on the bridge as in 2003; the audience would stay down below on the side of the field. No discussion.

REHEARSAL, DAY ONE

Despite my insistence in 2003 that I was not the boss and that the choreography would be initiated together with the drivers from point zero, the triennial staff did not really accept this way of working and saw it as too radical. I was still asked to begin by "explaining the plan" to the drivers and then immediately "move to practice." Practice what? I asked myself. Nothing is there yet. I responded immediately: "I need to work together with the drivers in collaboration; because they are the expert drivers, not me. It must come from them as much as it comes from me. This is why the piece was so successful last time. There is one difference this year, and that is that we did *Snow Workers' Ballet 2003*, so we have a prior experience. I would like to keep several items from 2003, which worked beautifully. I will explain what happened in 2003, but, as for this year, I need to work that out with the drivers . . . we must establish a working spirit."

I needed to prove that I meant this—that I am not the boss who tells them what to do. So I took a big chance. Most of the drivers did not know me. I needed to transfer a sense of individual authority and empowerment to each one from the beginning. The first day of rehearsals, I invited the drivers out onto the field with me and asked each driver individually to take his vehicle out into the ballet site, one driver at a time. I posed to each a challenging set of questions, "Can you please show us what your vehicle can do? Then can you show us something you always wanted to try, when no one was watching you, a fantasy in your imagination that you had while doing your regular work that you couldn't try? Take over half the field or even the whole field if you like. Please take as much time as you need." I also wanted the drivers to become a kind of audience for each other, and to move their relationship with the trucks away from regular work and into a new mode where each driver becomes a performer and everyone else is the audience.

Well, it took the whole day to get through all thirteen vehicles. I got some brand new ideas from them, especially when they acted out their fantasies, things I didn't know these trucks could do. But it took the whole bloody, precious, valuable day! I also saw, out of the corner of my eye, the other drivers sitting, walking around, talking, trapped by the heat and possibly a kind of boredom, watching the one in the field; and, as well, a national and a regional TV crew and city officials, watching the one driver alone on the field trying this and that. The pace was excruciating. By the end of the day, I was sure that I had forfeited and lost the time I needed to do a great work, and that I couldn't grab it back. I was utterly freaked out.

But after the actual performance of this ballet, in the midst of a dazzling feeling of success, one of the drivers told me that it was the gesture of giving each person a chance by giving each the whole field to himself that made them feel so important, and encouraged them to give it their all. And they did.

REHEARSAL, DAYS TWO, THREE, AND FOUR

Everyone wanted to do *The Tragic Love Story of Romeo and Juliet* again, even the new drivers. They just assumed we would do it, as if it were an ancient tradition! The boss picked who would be Romeo and who would be Juliet. The new Romeo had been a driver of a rotary in 2003. The other driver was new. Both were shy, reticent, and hesitant. Because the first Romeo and Juliet had been so terrific, I wondered if these drivers had the aggressive showmanship of the earlier Romeo and Juliet. We tried routine after routine. Finally, I thought they just had to do it their own way, and work it out on their own. They also had the big Juliet blade this time. They worked and worked, repeating and repeating. Each time, they got better

and closer, taking many risks of getting their blades so entangled that they would flip each other over. By the end of the two-and-a-half days, after many repetitions, everyone just stood there in silence while they went through their dance.

Mr. Fukuzaki, the boss and now the conductor, stayed on the field every minute, leading with a baton. He never entered a truck like his predecessor. He stood deep among or in front of the trucks, or sometimes popped up all the way across the field at the river's edge. He was a continual presence and worked like a demon, constantly in motion through every rehearsal and the performance itself.

The festival's coordinator, Yoji Tobita, managed everything. Everything was his concern, from drawing chalk lines again and again across the entire field, then redrawing them once again to try some other movement we came up with, to making sure everyone had something to drink in the beastly heat. He was extraordinary.

It was phenomenally and brutally hot; the temperature was continuously in the upper nineties Fahrenheit with unspeakable humidity. The trucks, outfitted only for the winter, were not air-conditioned. We worked almost eight hours each day in the relentless sun. The drivers, frying, kept working without complaint. Most of their heads and necks were swaddled in towels to catch endless gushing rivulets of sweat. Gallons of water, wheat tea, and barley tea disappeared as soon as they appeared.

Every minute, the videographer Araki was on the field, on the bridge, inside the vehicles, shooting. The site was alive with media. The Japanese TV crew stayed and shot all day long, every day, from the beginning of rehearsals through the performance. So did the regional Niigata TV station.

Azusa Ono, my spectacular, high-spirited interpreter/translator, was so involved in everything that she became a participant as well. There was a chain of communication. Usually I told her in English what I wanted, any changes that I thought would work better. She often instructed me to add a compliment along with my comments; I always agreed and then she talked to the boss in Japanese and he talked to the drivers. It was very important to me that neither Azusa nor I directly told the drivers what to do. I expressed my feeling or thinking to the boss through Azusa; then he passed it along. The process worked in reverse when they wanted to discuss something with me. We worked it out. Things were moving along well like that; I felt we all understood each other.

However, at one time, on the last day of rehearsal when I thought everything was just about set, there was an unusual amount of unsettled-sounding discussion going on among the drivers. I was standing on the side with Azusa and asked her, "What are the drivers saying?" That was the first time that I had actually asked what were they saying. She turned to me, laughed, and said, "I don't understand them. They are speaking a rural dialect, different Japanese than mine." So here we were, almost at the end of the second whole ballet I was creating with them, my *fourth* trip there, and I had never known that the drivers were not speaking the same Japanese to the boss or to the triennial staff! Only one person, the boss Mr. Fukuzaki, spoke both the Tokyo dialect and the local dialect. Besides myself, the Tokyo-based triennial staff had also needed a translator! To me, it made our successful choreographic communication together—however it happened—almost like a miracle!

DRESS REHEARSAL, EARLY ON THE DAY OF THE PERFORMANCE

It was so hot that the field had become a dust bowl—except I noticed drivers arriving with umbrellas. It had suddenly rained on the day of the performance in 2003. Not again. Fram Kitagawa had written that he invited me back because the weather would be better this time.

The dress rehearsal went beautifully, but the truck movements kicked up more and more dust, making it hard to see their synchronicity, their expertise. The ongoing live radio weather reports were saying definitely rain. We broke for lunch and as we emerged from the restaurant, there was a total cloudburst. Everyone reassured me it would be all right. "I can't stand this; I can't do this," I said to myself. Then the storm passed. And actually, it was a bonus, helping us by wetting down the field. The sun reemerged, warming everything. The colors became more vivid; everything sparkled with the clear light, huge puffy clouds, and spectacular sunset. We were blessed.

THE BALLET

MOVEMENT I: DEFINE THE BOUNDARIES OF THE SITE

The vehicles entered the long wide field, honking and moving at a very fast pace straight down the path next to the roped-off audience. With the truck windows open, the profiled faces of the drivers looking intently straight ahead, seemed very close as they were backlit from the late afternoon sun beaming through their cabs. The audience started cheering immediately, before the ballet had even really begun, as if long lost heroes had returned home—that shocked me. The thirteen vehicles traced the boundary of the entire field all the way down to the river, along its banks, and back, reeling out a huge image of the entire landscape we were all part of.

One by one, the trucks entered the movement's first lane for a *long snake*. It grew like a giant reptile stretching out along the length of the field, then turning at the end to form another lane going in the opposite direction all the way to the other end and yet turning to form a third lane going in the opposite direction. As more and more vehicles entered, as if the snake were constricting then swelling, they gradually filled three long lanes that ran parallel to each other and to the audience. By the time all thirteen vehicles were on the field, they were crossing each other perfectly, from lane to lane, aligned across all three lanes. This happened at three different points within each lane, with incredible timing. It was difficult to synchronize hitting their crossing points at the same moment because the rotaries and the dozers were different lengths and moved differently. They looked as if they had become one sinuous animal.

MOVEMENT II: DANCE OF THE TIRE DOZERS: THE TRAGIC LOVE STORY OF ROMEO AND JULIET

This time, Juliet entered the field entirely alone, independent, weaving slowly this way and that, exploring her new world on her own, unafraid. Romeo followed her carefully, giving her time, then caught up next to her. They proceeded together, so close their wheels looked as it they would touch as they circled in the same direction before they separated in order to face each other in the center of the field. The chorus of dozers entered from the other corner of the field and circled the couple, guarding them from outside, showing off their dazzling blade powers together.

Romeo and Juliet now completely owned the tragedy. It was hard to believe that their blade motions could become so varied, expressing so many emotions: curiosity in seeking and investigating each other; Juliet's sudden shyness and blade-down retreat, then, tipping her blade upward, her forthright tender declaration of love, led to an enveloping kiss where Romeo put his butterfly blades so closely around Juliet it was breathtaking; and finally ecstasy as they raised their blades to heaven, unafraid. Then they added something no one knew these trucks could do. They vibrated. Both entire vehicles shook at the same time as their blades were almost touching! This was straight-out sensuous, funny, and sexy. The audience went wild!

The contrapuntal dynamic between their intensity in the center of the field and the synchronized movements of the yellow, green, and red tire-dozer chorus, tilting this way and that, rising, dipping down, swaying, positioned first on one side of the couple, then running around to play directly to the audience on the edge of the field—abandoning the couple—was dramatic, even operatic. And Motor Grader! Mr. Yanagi, amplifying what he did in 2003, was fierce, absolutely shameless, slanting his wheels almost horizontally to the ground, zooming in on the couple, horn blaring away, zooming through the couple, very scary, forcing them to separate. Romeo and Juliet kept coming back together, heedless. Motor Grader charged through them again and again and finally forced them to abandon the field entirely, defeated, blades dragging. The crowd roared angrily! Then the tiny baby rotary, defiantly ignoring the great size difference between them, blazed ahead and chased Motor Grader this way and that, back and forth across the field until Motor Grader, too, was defeated and vanished.

MOVEMENT III: DANCE OF THE ROTARIES

After the fiery emotions of Romeo and Juliet, this move, the *zigzag*, with its calm synchronicity and geometric exactness, was like a refreshing drink of cool water. All six big rotaries, three by three, wheels almost touching, led by Baby Rotary, bunched up extremely close together. Moving as one unit, they made a huge zigzag from one corner of the field near the audience to the midpoint across the field at the river's edge, then shifting on a sharp angle, they cut diagonally back to the other corner of the field, again near the audience.

All the rotaries then lined up in the middle of the field for the *rotaries shooters' dance*, twirling one after the other, and came very close to the audience to face them directly. Some manipulated their swing-ogre blades, others their chopping blades. Then all together, they raised their shooters and showed what they could do, including wagging their "heads" in a gesture that looked as if they were saying "NO NO NO," then turning in the shooters to face the drivers through the window and laying down to go to sleep. These shooters, in the winter, suck up the snow that the mighty rotary blades swallow, shooting them in beautiful plumes off to the side of the streets like white fountains, or into the waiting dump trucks that take the snow to be dumped in the river, endlessly throughout the winter. This movement ended when the rotaries raised themselves unexpectedly, as if standing on tip-toe, and whirled their massive spiral blades, spinning them as fast as possible, roaringly fast, so powerful, so close to the audience, and then stopping suddenly, as if they had become something else, all the vehicles tipped slightly to the left and then to the right as if they were curtsying.

MOVEMENT IV: FINALE

All thirteen vehicles participated in the three moves for the finale. For the first part, while studying the long video passages shot by our videographer Araki during the previous winter's snow work that he had sent to me in New York City, I was mesmerized by how the tire dozer, in the endless cycles of collecting and dumping snow, wiggled its rear end and rear wheels to get a stable grip on uneven frozen mounds of snow while, at the same time, shaking its bucket up front, in a different rhythm and trajectory, continuing to shift then dump the heap, then pushing the snow over the edge of the hill going down to the Shinano River, the same river that was next to the "stage" of the ballet. The worker could move the truck differently in the back than in the front through a joint in the middle that enabled it to be quite flexible, as if two different vehicles were operating in one body. I was very impressed by the machine's flexibility as it worked in the midst of frigid snowfalls and mounds of rigid solid snow as far as one could see. This flexibility, which I thought was the mark of an intelligent work system, was called *nakaore*, and I wanted to show it in the ballet.[1]

I discussed this with the drivers and they liked that I noticed this refinement in their vehicles and in their work. We decided to feature it for the first part of the finale. Everyone, all thirteen vehicles, went to the river's edge, backs to the audience, and spread out across the length of the field. Slowly, together, each one showed this *nakaore* aspect by moving the

---

1   In Japanese, the word *nakaore* refers to a soft felt hat with its center folded inside. When applied to a big hard vehicle like a snow truck, it means that it can move its front section separately from its rear section, thus exhibiting unexpected flexibility.

back differently from the front and then wiggling and wagging the back, doing a kind of can-can movement, each different kind of vehicle doing it differently, while they all moved backward very slowly toward the audience, to the middle of the field. They called it *kune kune back*, which might have had an illicit overtone, like "wiggle your ass." It was a surprising and very funny move.

The second move: From the midline of the field, they all made a slow Noh dance turn, and came toward the audience, with each vehicle signaling to the audience in its own way: blades sliding, tipping, going up and down, shooters waving, horns blaring, the drivers making whatever signals to the audience from their truck that they wanted until they came right up to the edge of the audience. Then they stopped.

The third move was *long diagonal*. As in 2003, the drivers backed into position and formed an extremely long diagonal that articulated the length and depth of the field, and then stopped. It became a still landscape sculpture. Then each driver got out of his truck, stood in front of it, took off his safety hat, and took a bow.

I was sitting with the audience throughout the performance. At this point I walked up and down the roped path, inviting the audience through hand gestures to come across the field to join the drivers. I had been advised, "Since Japanese people are very shy, they will never do this." The energy level was so intense and positive that I tried anyhow. The advice was incorrect. Many adults and children jumped at the chance and streamed across the field, racing to meet the drivers, shaking their hands, climbing into the trucks' cabs, pretending to drive, and getting a ride on the rising and falling blades. I was taken by how many women climbed into the drivers' seats! (No driver in Echigo-Tsumari is a woman, yet.) It was a joyous outpouring!

As I walked among the drivers, going from driver to driver as each was standing in front of his vehicle, scanning the landscape with all the vehicles spread out across the whole field on *the long diagonal*, I felt a growing sense of triumph rolling from person to person. Even in the midst of the happy, noisy, jostling crowd, a kind of majestic calm surrounded each driver. It seemed as if the personal power that each earned and owned in the winter, often working alone, was quietly vibrating. And then, each walked away from his own truck and joined the other drivers, the festival staff and me. The palpability of our joint accomplishment—that this audience was showing such tremendous ap-

preciation for—rose up. We knew that we made this and we knew that we did it together.

AFTER THE FIRST PERFORMANCE

I couldn't stay for more than the first performance. It was so hard to be away from a work that had moved into my soul. Over the next two months, I worried about everything and kept in touch about the second and third performances with the Echigo Tsumari staff and my video team who were also still working. Then in November 2012, after the third performance in September, an account from my translator Azousa Ono arrived. Here are some excerpts:

What Mierle wanted from drivers during the creating process was that she wanted them to live in their fantasy world. Driving the snowplow trucks must have been a very serious job for them. So was Mierle. She was very keen to expand the world of snow and the world of snowplow driver in the middle of summer, which was absolutely novelty. In a way, Mierle carefully tickled drivers' desire to play in/outside of their work place in order to draw out their personalities through their trucks. . . .

The direction of Mierle was very precise, playful and delicate. I've never seen someone who is in love with machines so much as if loving in human. Once the trucks have personalities they become individuals. The group movement (unison) done by individuals was a very strong image.

The metaphor of vitality between human and nature. The inseparable interaction between human and machine. The time contrast between summer and winter. The different environment between countryside and city. Those important factors of her piece made us realize something we are missing in our consciousness in every day's life. Especially in such difficult time in Japan after the big earthquake, tsunami, tempest, land slidings one after other, I as a Japanese felt very emotional to see those drivers working very hard for us and putting their life on the risk. . . . At same time I felt exhilarating to see the drivers enjoying and exploring their machines in the big peaceful field as they want in the Mierle's piece.

. . . I was so moved when I saw the audience walking/running towards the drivers with full of smile and excitement (they looked like a big wave of tsunami!) at the end of the show. The local audience as well as outsiders absolutely loved their heroes and they were proud of them.

I think this performance will stay on my heart forever and it made me a strong attachment to this snow region. It made me feel like going there while they have snow.

Dance of the Dozers: The Tragic Love Story of Romeo and Juliet

Preparation and rehearsal

Long Snake

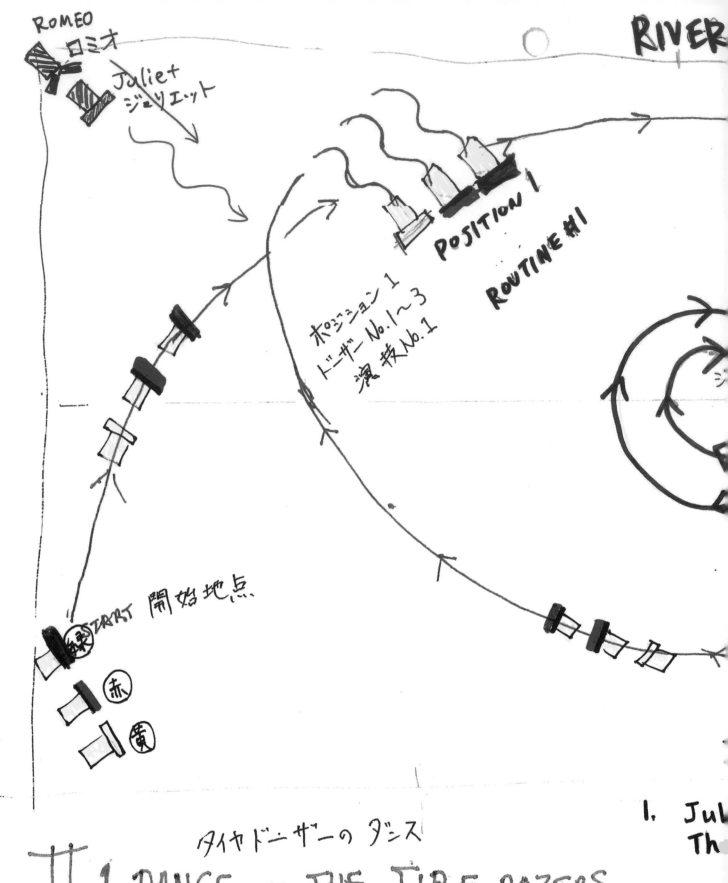

ROMEO
ロミオ

Juliet
ジュリエット

RIVER

POSITION 1
ROUTINE #1

ポジション 1
ドーザー No.1～3
演技 No.1

START 開始地点

録
赤
黄

タイヤドーザーの ダンス

Ⅱ.1. DANCE of THE TIRE DOZERS
ROMEO & JULIET
ロミオとジュリエット

1. Jul
Th

2. 3
cir
w

2. タイヤドーザ

Drawing of choreography

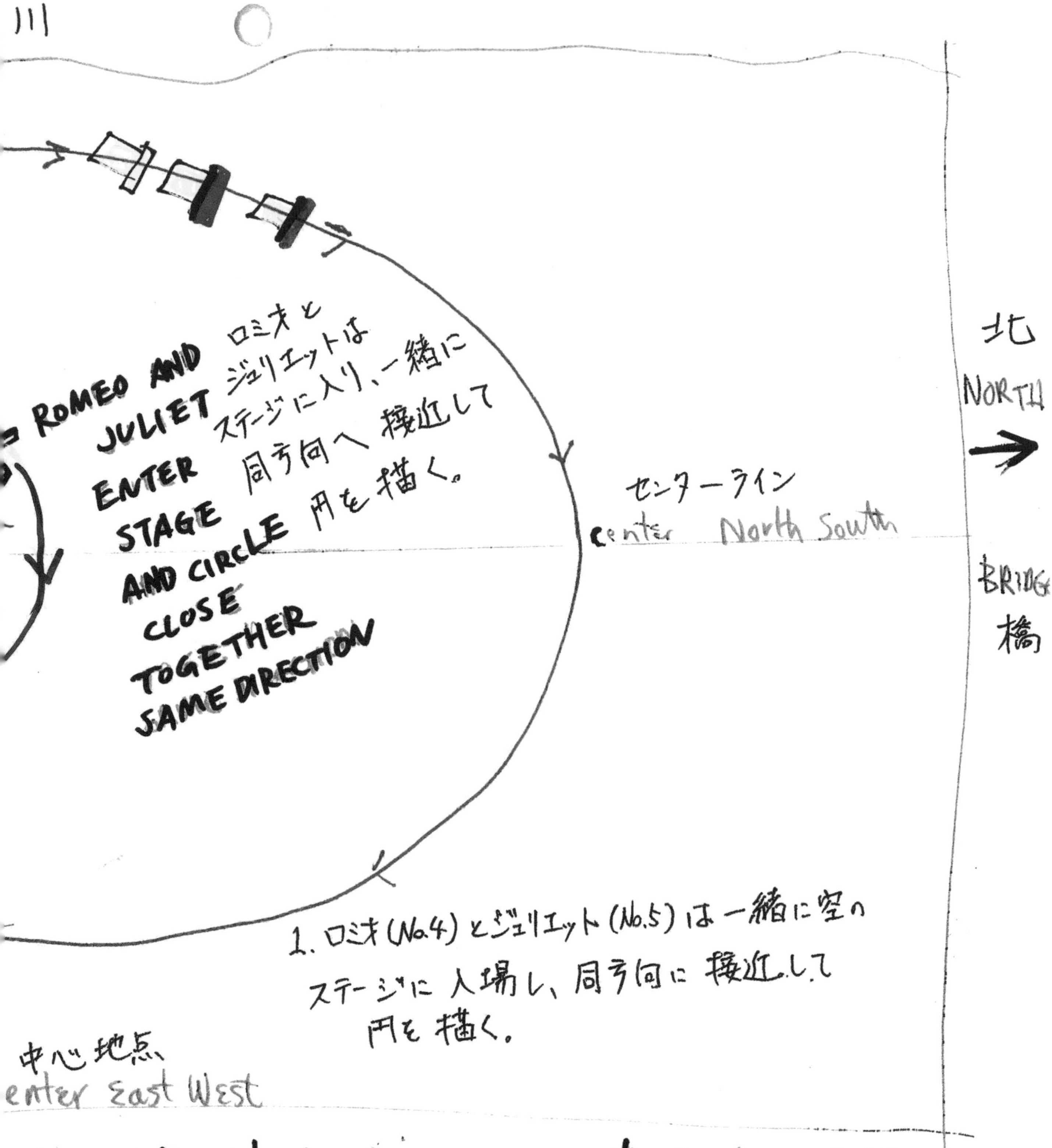

川 ◯

ROMEO AND ロミオと
JULIET ジュリエットは
ENTER ステージに入り、一緒に
STAGE 同方向へ接近して
AND CIRCLE 円を描く。
CLOSE
TOGETHER
SAME DIRECTION

センターライン
center North South

北
NORTH →

BRIDG
橋

1. ロミオ(No.4)とジュリエット(No.5)は一緒に空の
   ステージに入場し、同方向に接近して
   円を描く。

中心地点
enter East West

enters followed by Romeo   to EMPTY STAGE.
ircle close together, same direction

DOZERS   single file, make medium big
single file, go to SOUTH WEST CORNER DIAGONAL
in & take position #1
台は 1列で中くらいの円を描き、南西コーナーからジグザグに
ポジション 1 へ移動する。
(~3)

The kiss

Chorus abandons Romeo and Juliet to play to the audience

Motor Grader sneaking by the couple

Motor Grader forces the couple apart and destroys their future

Baby Rotary vanquishes Motor Grader

Dance of the Rotaries: Rotaries Shooters' Dance

Finale: *Come to the Audience and Bow*

Finale: *Long Diagonal*

After the ballet the audience rushes to the drivers and the vehicles

The thirteen drivers of *Snow Workers' Ballet 2012*

CREDITS AND DETAILS

SNOW WORKERS' BALLET 2012

DATE AND TIME

July 30, 2012 (first performance)
5:00–6:00 p.m.

August 18, 2012 (second performance)
5:00–6:00 p.m.

September 15, 2012 (third performance)
4:30–5:30 p.m.

August 3–September 17, 2012
Video installation

LOCATION

Tokamachi, Niigata Prefecture, Japan

SITE

The ballet took place alongside the Shinano River on a field 150 meters long and 75 meters wide.
The video installation, drawings, and photographic portraits of the drivers were shown at the Kinare, which
had become the Echigo-Tsumari Satoyama Museum of Contemporary Arts.

Tokamachi had a population of 59,000 in 2012 and the most snowfall on Japan's main island of Honshu
among cities of its size and larger.

INVITING INSTITUTION, STAFF, AND OFFICIALS

Echigo-Tsumari Triennial 2012:
Fram Kitagawa, General Director
Toshio Kondo, International Artist Project Coordinator
Yoji Tobita, Project Manager of *Snow Workers' Ballet*
Sachi Yanadori, Assistant Manager
Azusa Ono, Translator

Tokamachi City Office:
Hidenobu Oketani, Manager
Akira Ishii, Assistant Manager

MOVEMENTS

Movement I: *Define the Boundaries of the Site* and *Long Snake*
Movement II: *Dance of the Dozers: The Tragic Love Story of Romeo and Juliet*
Movement III: *Dance of the Rotaries: Zigzag* and *Rotaries Shooters' Dance*
Movement IV: Finale: *Nakaore: Kune Kune Back*, *Come to the Audience*, and *Long Diagonal*

VEHICLES AND DRIVERS

Thirteen snow vehicles:
Three large tire dozers with red, green, and yellow blades
One large tire dozer with peach blade, "Juliet"
One large tire dozer with purple blade, "Romeo"
Six large rotaries
One baby rotary
One motor grader

Supervisor and conductor:
Mitsugi Fukuzaki

Drivers of large snow tire dozers:
Hirohiko Nogami, "Romeo," purple blade
Noriyoshi Kuwabara, "Juliet," peach blade
Shigekatsu Takahashi, red blade
Nisaku Ikeda, green blade
Masashi Kuwahara, yellow blade

Driver of the motor grader:
Haruyoshi Yanagi

Drivers of the rotaries (including different drivers for the second and third performances):
Kakichi Ichikawa
Kazuyoshi Kosugi
Nobuyuki Mizuochi (also painter of the blades)
Yuichi Muruyama
Koji Niwano
Masayoshi Sakai
Masayuki Takano
Tadashi Watabe
Yoshihiro Yanagi

DOCUMENTATION

Video:
Takahisa Araki, Videographer
Tomoko Uesugi, Editor

Photography:
Yasuhisa Ishii
Osamu Nakamura
Hiroshi Noguchi

AUDIENCE

The audience was alongside the southeastern edge of the field on the same level as the vehicles, separated by a path and guard ropes. The audience numbered 400 for the first performance, 650 for the second, and 1,700 for the third.

MIERLE LADERMAN UKELES IN CONVERSATION WITH TOM FINKELPEARL AND SHANNON JACKSON

TF: The other day I was walking along and saw sanitation workers who were taking this *big* pile of plastic bags filled with garbage into their truck. And one of the guys had this special 360-degree turn, where he would pick the thing up and turn it all the way around and throw it in.

MLU: That's a good guy.

TF: Yes, it was *very* beautiful but also *only* visible to me because of your work.

MLU: He was riding the wave . . .

TF: And the younger guy was just throwing the bags in there. So you are giving me an aesthetic view of an ordinary process on the street. It might sound funny, but in the actual moment it was beautiful. In terms of the element of humor in your work, when you actually go to the performances, it's a little different from hearing them described. When you're telling someone about a ballet for garbage barges or snow-removal vehicles people kind of laugh at the verbal disjuncture—I think Freud speaks about the cruelty of humor. So, people laugh when you say a ballet for garbage barges because they don't think of garbage barges as being balletic; they think there's something absurd. I think the absurdity comes from prejudice around social class. But when you are at the performance, people laugh because they see something brilliant and cool, in an unexpected way.

MLU: And there's a feeling of separation from the members of the audience who laugh because they can't get across the bridge of a worker having the grace of a dancer.

TF: Once you get the performance, the audience is laughing *with* them, not against them. During and after the performance the audience thinks it is amazing.

SJ: One way of thinking about the humor is that it might be the effect of the juxtaposition you have said you are going for. In chapter one, you write about creating a space of freedom within a space of necessity. There is something about joining "artist-in-residence" with "department of sanitation"—or about joining ballet to garbage trucks—that creates an unexpected juxtaposition within what you call that space of necessity. The artistic frame loosens things up. And sometimes the reaction to that artistic gesture could be laughter. That humor might be a way of prompting a re-imagination of a whole lot of other things.

MLU: Well, I am very interested in the re-imagination of necessity.

SJ: Even when someone calls it humorous?

MLU: It is humorous but it is also dead serious because I really tried to burst things open. We are innately free creatures, but we live in a world of finite resources that brings with it many constraints. What do we do with that disjuncture? It makes us chafe so much, because freedom and necessity don't fit together smoothly. One thing that I think is so necessary to protect our freedom, especially in a democratic culture, is to always test and push back when anybody says you have to do something. You always have the right to ask why, or to propose another way. Now for the people who do the endless work of necessity, you always have to ask, is that the way you *have* to do it? Also know that inside each of those people, there's a hell of a lot more than the job lets you understand about the whole person.

TF: But, in order to get somebody to open their mind, like the audience, sometimes humor is shared. It's a very powerful tool. And I don't think that you should feel defensive about it.

MLU: Well, the Romeo and Juliet segment of the *Snow Workers' Ballet 2003* has humor, I fully understood that. For example, the tiny baby rotary chasing the great big fearsome motor grader off the field, driving him crazy—I put that humor in there.

TF: But you know it is funny because it is also original, right? If you say, "I am a landscape painter," there's nothing funny about that because it is so predictable. "I'm a painter, I do landscapes."

MLU: Unless you see that landscapes are so weird . . .

TF: Well then painting can be funny, but your position as an artist is not. We have known each other for a long time and I've described your work and almost every time I describe your work I get a chuckle, still! But by now it's not a negative. It's like, "Oh my god, that's possible!"

SJ: Coming from theater, we often think about Bertolt Brecht's attempts at defamiliarization—or what is often translated as "alienation"—to get theater audiences to imagine a new sense of social possibility. He often felt that social criticism was linked to laughter, that laughter was a first step toward a kind of criticality. I understand what Mierle is saying; laughter can be dismissive. But I think it is so much about what happens in the next step after this initial unfamiliar juxtaposition. After laughter, what happens? Is there a kind of critical thinking or deeper understanding of an individual or a worker that you never really had before?

TF: Mindy Thompson Fullilove, a Columbia University psychiatry professor, talks about how Jane Jacobs used the word "ballet" to describe putting the garbage out on the street in her 1961 book *The Death and Life of Great American Cities*. Here is the quote: "In using 'ballet' to describe the prosaic acts of putting out the garbage and nodding to the fruit seller, Jane Jacobs challenged us to open our senses and our understanding. She was well aware that the scene she described was imperiled by urban renewal precisely because it was devalued by power brokers interested in other uses for the land. Her reframing 'putting out the garbage' as 'sidewalk ballet' created a weapon

protecting neighborhoods."[1] To me the disjuncture is still of the word "ballet" and putting it next to the street ballet or the urban ballet or the ballet mécanique, so it's not completely outside of modernist traditions.

SJ: To take the ballet theme in a slightly different direction—I think that the concept is interesting, not just because it is a high-class art form, but also because it is a performance form. To me, deciding to call the waking city a ballet really brings out different associations; it reminds us that the city is a space of coordination and choreography, an ensemble of parts moving and functioning together. The sense of group ensemble is really a different kind of analogy to performance. In fact, I was really struck reading through your whole text by how many performance metaphors and performance connections you have throughout the book. You talk about the parade, about the bodily comportment of the stooped street sweeper, and about how many performance festivals have offered you certain opportunities to do your work. The performance aspect is about a kind of coordination, coordinating large operations of people, objects, and machines in a different way. It might not be what people first think of when they hear this word "ballet," but the idea of choreography seems to have much wider associations beyond the classed ones.

MLU: I agree with you a hundred percent because the term ballet might shrink the wider associations of performance.

SJ: It *risks* doing that, but there are so many other performances. It was so interesting to me that what you are covering in this book are not only works that were called ballet, the ballet mécanique, but so many other works that for you have a link to a choreographic imagination. So the link to performance is wide and deep, and also quite complex.

MLU: Thank you. I mean, it's true and I am nervous about using the word. I've used the word in *Snow Workers' Ballet* or in *Marrying the Barges: A Barge Ballet* (1984). It was easy, rather than other bigger, longer words.

SJ: Can you speak about these other performance associations—linked to the gestures of the workers and the use of the word "choreography." What are the personal resonances that those kinds of terms have for you?

MLU: In *Movin' On Along* (1992) I developed a choreography with retired steel workers for our performance work based on the gestures that they had invented to use with each other on the work floor in the steel mill. These gestures were not casual or random. Because the work floor was extremely noisy, they couldn't hear each other. It was a very dangerous work situation with tons of steel being moved up and down and sideways all the time, so they had to pay very close attention to what was happening. The only way to do this was through their gestures. We took their energetic gestures for "Take it up," "Bring it down," "Move it sideways," "Watch it!" and used them outside to express their hopes and dreams in relation to the barges filled with recycled steel, even though their steel mills had gone bankrupt, and really, they felt, had abandoned them and their many health concerns. Making this a public "choreography" was quite natural.

Also, when I was learning about the New York City Department of Sanitation, which I always just call "sanitation" or "DSNY," I immersed myself for a year and half in research because I really didn't know very much about sanitation at all—other than my feeling that I had luckily fallen into the major leagues of the maintenance world. Even though I had been dealing with maintenance systems at smaller scales for over a decade by then, as far as what sanitation is, what do they do, where they are and all that, I knew very little. The closest word to me about aiming to deal with the wholeness of this entire system and also to a notion of performance or choreography is actually "operations."[2]

SJ: Yes, great. I love that word.

MLU: Operations engages the entire city: that's what I was privileged to learn in planning *Touch Sanitation*, my first citywide performance work where I faced and shook hands with all the 8,500 sanitation workers in New York City from 1977 to 1980, and said to each, "Thank you for keeping New York City alive." I insisted that for my work to deal with the entire system of sanitation and all the workers, my performance artwork had to occur throughout the entire system, in every single facility. It could not be accomplished, like a social scientist's study, via a representative sample of sanitation. The way I learned was always through a notion of piggybacking, asking, "How does sanitation deal with the whole city?" How do the central officials downtown, at the main headquarters or borough headquarters, connect with the entire city? How do they do this? It's like an army.

SJ: So interesting to try to think about how an art project could expose this systemic connection.

MLU: How do they connect to the sanitation worker walking down the street in Queens? And that is the question. That Jane Jacobs image—it's the same thing. It's a total choreography of this coordination of performance, and actually . . .

SJ: An ensemble of component parts . . .

MLU: Yes! Because my image, and I am happy to say this here, because I think that the underlying image in my work is always sort of a big system image, and I don't know if that's generally understood. You know I get marginalized as a happy house worker, or something like that, but my interest, along with the worker, is *the city*. How does the city work? And sanitation is such a great way to learn about the city because they are experts at this *incredible scale of coordination*. And also the virtues that I learned around service workers that seemed so alien to my training as an artist or even my interests as an artist, which were primarily to be unfettered, to be free to do whatever I wanted. Whereas for the people who are doing this kind of work continually over the long span of their work lives, the virtues are different: endurance, a kind of calm, decision making often in the midst of chaos. When some hell breaks loose, and it's always breaking loose—garbage really has a mind of its own—so when that happens, it's called a "condition." When I would hear a sanitation worker calling his superintendent on the phone, saying, "Super, we have a condition"—such a calm word—it could really mean horrifying things like a truck blew up, we have garbage all over the street, it's all over the people, people are hysterical. There's this calm, they don't run away, they hang in there and deal with it. And I really learned to love that. Actually it has a connection to me at the deepest personal level— when you have a baby and maybe three sick kids and you're exhausted out of your mind. And you're really done and your brain is jumping out of your head and

1   Mindy Thompson Fullilove, "The Logic of Small Pieces: A Story in Three Ballets," in *What We See: Advancing the Observations of Jane Jacobs*, ed. Stephen Arthur Goldsmith and Lynne Elizabeth (Oakland, CA: New Village Press, 2010), 75–76.
2   Krzysztof Wodiczko referred to Ukeles's work in terms of "operations" when he said, "Ukeles's body of work is exemplary as a reactualization of the avant-garde tradition, the one represented by Soviet artists of Productivism, Constructivism, even Proletkult—what Walter Benjamin called the 'author as producer,' an 'operational' artist." From his introduction to Ukeles's lecture at the Harvard Graduate School of Design, Cambridge, February 12, 2013.

you just have to find some way to calm down and not lose it too bad.

SJ: I feel that it is really clear in this book, the sense that it's about operations and systems. We often see you marveling at how the operations kind of click into place to solve issues, including issues that come up in the course of your artwork. Another thing that really struck me is how the inspiration for the structures of your art pieces comes from being inside a sanitation process. You were watching the droppings being swept and that prompted you to think differently about what a parade could be. Or you were sitting inside the truck and seeing the chaos all around the workers, thinking that some day you would create a clear space so that these trucks and workers could do what they want. Which led to the first ballet . . .

MLU: The sweeper—sitting inside the sweeper. Right.

SJ: Yes, or then you really wanting to understand how push boats work, and to think about what it means to move in an opposite direction.

MLU: Totally. It's a different task.

SJ: So much of the technical and aesthetic structure comes from inside the operation. I don't think I really had a sense of how deep that was until now.

TF: In reading your texts throughout the book, something that kept coming up was repeated anxiety: starting the preparations and thinking, "I don't think that this is going to work this time. We only have three days!" But the side by side of that is patience. You *have* to let it unfold, right? You only had three days for rehearsals, but you spent a whole day just watching to see what people could do. Of course if you hadn't been patient enough to let it unfold it wouldn't have been a proper representation of what these men were capable of doing.[3]

MLU: There's so much anxiety in having only three days and not knowing what will happen! One has to ask, do you always work like that? Or would you always have to get yourself into situations like that? The fact is, I always thought that if I did a really good ballet, the next time someone invited me, they would say, "How many days would you actually like?" [*laughter*] and then I would say, "Three weeks, I would like three weeks!" To have the time to try this or that,

I mean to *really* try it. I could have used more days, and *they* could have used more days also. So actually this three-day thing, however it's arranged, is like a commission at a certain level, and in that commission there's a value judgment that it's worth *that* much. That the system will invest only that much and the fact that, even to this day there is not someone banging on the table saying, "Let her have two weeks!" or, "Ask her, don't tell her!" The money is always squeezed out; it's the minimum.

TF: I don't agree with that.

MLU: You don't?

TF: No. Here's why. Every commission by every artist always has a budget. And your budgets are completely invisible, they're in-kind.

MLU: Right.

TF: These are much bigger budgets than what most artists are dealing with. You received a million pounds of glass at the Museum of Contemporary Art in Los Angeles.[4] No artist has ever done that since then. You did it in-kind. The museum budget did not pay for the materials or labor. In Japan, you got thirteen drivers with thirteen vehicles driving around for three days— that's a lot of money.

MLU: Right. It is a lot—I am fully aware that it is a lot of money. But I'm usually focusing on gauging my in-kind request in relation to the scale of the real-world work system, so that the art in relation to that scale makes a kind of real-world work-system sense. So I'm often focusing on how big, how much, how many is the norm in the real-world system, not what usually appears "normal" scale in art-world institutions.

TF: So do you ever calculate these things? I remember seeing that there were thousands of hours donated by the city for your Los Angeles piece.

MLU: Well, because I had to negotiate with the city how many hours they would give me.

TF: Do you ever multiply that out, times their wages?

MLU: No.

TF: I'm sure that's a lot of money. I'm just saying

everything has constraints. You're working on a *large scale* . . .

MLU: I've accepted that.

TF: So, I'm just saying, from the point of view of the art world . . .

MLU: It's not nothing . . .

TF: Okay, right.

MLU: It's not nothing. I don't want to sound ungrateful and all that. But this anxiety thing, it's tough! It's really scary. It's genuinely very scary. But, I must say to myself, looking back, the first time (I didn't know this in advance) I just sort of did it out of what I needed as an artist and that's to let myself do my work.

Not have somebody tell me what to do. So the very first time we met, in 1983, for the *Ballet Mécanique for Six Mechanical Sweepers* on Randall's Island in New York City, they gave us three day's rehearsal. I had never done anything like that before, and I walked into the supervisor's empty shack on the edge of the training field—these people didn't know each other, I didn't know them. And they said, "Tell us what to do."

And the bell rang in my head—you know, as an artist, I'm not from that world, I'm different and I'm here to do something different with you. And I said, "No, I'm not the boss, I want us to do this together. I have some ideas, but I really admire your work and your skill. I have driven around, I have seen what you do." My job is to clear the way so people can see you. And then it went silent.

SJ: Yeah, that was so revealing—the anxiety of wondering whether this was going to work.

MLU: Tick, tick, tick, tick, tick, tick—the three-day clock is ticking. I'm saying to myself, "You jerk, this is going to be the biggest flop! And you'll be out of there, Ukeles. What are you doing? This is crazy!" But, that is how I would be as an artist when you go all by yourself into the studio and you're in this vacuum. It really is the same thing. There is also this belief that everybody has a lot of stuff that they would really like to try out. And art is the excuse. It is!

SJ: Yes, absolutely. I think that's what you're talking about when you said you get your three-day commis-

sion and try to figure out how you can push that more. I feel like those kinds of questions about how to create space for allowing co-participants to decide what they want to do really is striking. You were dealing with it earlier in 1979, but now I think that question is on the minds of so many different socially engaged artists and art institutions. They want to commission social engagement, but the parameters of the commission and the available time frame really start to become a challenge. I think it is more on the minds of everyone, now. The runway toward an art event might need a kind of different support structure, something more than your typical three-day installation.

TF: I want to get back to what Shannon said before because I think it's fundamental. This whole question of the view from inside, from inside the truck or inside the sanitation department—you have been there for more than thirty-five years?

SJ: Yes, I love that . . .

MLU: Since 1977. It's distressing for the projects that I think I could have finished that I'm still working on. "Deferred maintenance," as Shannon has called it.[5]

TF: Just being there on an everyday basis, all the time, means that you are viewing things from a different perspective. Viewing things from inside the truck and understanding what flows out of that naturally.

MLU: There is also my being able to develop an intense kind of visceral and emotional response to the sometimes-unfair public reaction toward the sanitation worker inside that truck or even toward the boss at headquarters, not unlike what the worker himself feels. It's been a great privilege to learn a lot about a citywide infrastructure system—it's like a lens to see the whole city that enables you to get an understanding of the city. I think it's an important kind of education. I wish a lot of people would have a more holistic understanding of when you say something's necessary to really understand it. The durational aspect of trying to deal with certain heavy at-scale content matter is really

3　All the drivers in the seven ballets were men.
4　*Unburning Freedom Hall*, including *Peacetalks at the Hearth*, installation for "Uncommon Sense," curated by Julie Lazar and Tom Finkelpearl, Museum of Contemporary Art, Los Angeles, March 16–July 6, 1997.
5　See Shannon Jackson, "High Maintenance: The Sanitation Aesthetics of Mierle Laderman Ukeles," chap. 3 of *Social Works: Performing Art, Supporting Publics* (New York: Routledge, 2011).

quite demanding and quite long. And what Shannon said, as more institutions are interested in this, it must be a little scary to them.

SJ: Constant expressions of anxiety.

MLU: If it's not a coherent object that will be produced, where is the responsibility of the commissioning institution? Here this artist is moving in! And there she still is! And she wants to speak with you, more than once!

TF: One of things you mentioned in relationship to the *Re-Spect For Givors* (1993) project—at the very end the maid at the hotel knocks on your door and says, "You did a great job." She was the wife of the guy who originally said, "We get no respect." So there's this implication at some level of a positive psychological outcome for the guy who is feeling more respected. There is a social value. The workers, for at least the moment or perhaps long term, got a little bit more respect. So what's that about? Does that make the project in Givors more successful? As an art project? As a social project? What about the balance between the social value and the artistic outcome that day in Givors?

MLU: That's a great question. What if it had been a mediocre artwork, or even a sort of junky artwork, but maybe the workers at a certain level would get a kind of social benefit just from being seen, even kind of highlighted, when the way was cleared so people could actually look at them? But, for me, it had to be a terrific artwork beyond that, or it would just be awful. For me, the way it became good art is because—going all the way back to my first insight—setting out to make the art together opened a gate for the individual worker to be able to enter, to cocreate or co-imagine, this work. They already had the skill before—that is why I wanted to work with them. To me, the value of the art was that it could arise in the unknown, even wild space between us. It became something that simply didn't exist before. That made it a good artwork. Of course, that also has social value.

SJ: When you speak about co-creation and the creation of space between you and the workers that didn't exist before, to me the social effect has aesthetic value. That the effect in the social realm is part of the aesthetic act, that it is integral to the aesthetic act. Rather than it being conceived as a trade-off between

being a "good artwork" or having "good social effects," it's like saying, "No, actually this social interaction is the aesthetic material."

MLU: I agree with you, but I think you have to ask why. I feel that the reason why is because you're looking at freedom. As a result of our working in an atmosphere of freedom, something new can arise between everyone there, when we all come together and create this thing together. Freedom is what makes it possible. That's terrific. The social value is more about freedom than social morals or something like that.

SJ: Right.

TF: In discussions with my sister, who is a classicist, she told me that in ancient Western aesthetics there was a value on skill, realism, and beauty. I feel that postmodern aesthetics have more to do with complexity, openness, and a relationship with artistic tradition. In your ballets, I think I have seen all six aesthetic elements. There's beauty, realism (in a material sense), and skill, but not only your skill, often the skill of the collaborators and then complexity, openness, and a relationship with tradition like the *ballet mécanique*, modern performance traditions. Compared to *Touch Sanitation*, or some of your other work, the ballets are a bit more traditional in aesthetic terms . . .

MLU: I'm not sure about that.

TF: They were beautiful, they were choreographed, actions unfolded. You described it in the narrative the beauty and the skill. I think that there is skill in *Touch Sanitation* . . .

MLU: The skill was in trying to design how to map a city as a performance.

TF: I understand that, but if you talk to your average guy on the street and say, "Oh, she shook hands with 8,500 people." It's very hard to get them to understand that as art. But the ballets might be more accessible to the public than some of your more conceptual performance pieces.

MLU: Maybe they do have an easier beginning, middle, and end. I think that's pleasurable. Rather than a performance work that could go on for a year—

TF: Or thirty-five years—

MLU: —or whatever, thirty-five years—it's not so pleasurable.

TF: But here I would postulate that the beginning isn't the beginning like the hour or two-hour performance—the beginning is your first meeting with the workers and the end is when the last vestige of the feeling of respect vanishes from the workers' psyches.

MLU: I agree. Let's not let go of the social aspect quite so easily. The original ballet mécanique or the notions of engaging masses of workers in art had a fabulous revolutionary spirit about it: the notion of the worker as the culture-maker. I feel that my work comes out of that and I want my work understood as coming out of that early revolutionary stream. But there is also a sort of dangerous confusion when people and machines get too close: Are people machines? At times, the machinelike movements that people were messing around with could have a kind of totalitarian edge where masses of people became manipulated and digested by the machine of the state. Which is actually what ended up happening out of the incredibly explosive early utopian Russian revolutionist art that got imprisoned in mass-controlled choreographies from the late 1920s to the 1940s.

But, when you asked if it has social value—I don't want to let go of that. Because I think it has to do with trying to communicate that if we decide that we *have* to do certain things to stay alive in the city, and to survive on the planet, then we *have* to have a way in our culture to see the people that are doing the endless tasks that make this possible. In Western culture, it's very hard for people to continue to see these systems and the people that are working like that, and the meaning of it. It's even hard for the people inside the systems themselves to get a sense of the whole scale.

TF: I saw that just by hanging out in the sanitation department with you. Where people would say, "Hey, face it, I'm a garbage man."

MLU: Right, like make them small.

TF: Almost as if they had internalized that fear in themselves.

MLU: Right. Well, that is an evil thing that happens in work systems all over. "I'm just a blah, blah, blah." And I just really want to bash that open.

SJ: There is a historic connection between your work and the Constructivist legacy of coordinating workers' theater and of using labor as inspiration for art making. There's also the effort to refuse the binary between art and social value or art and labor. Those are all things that I think are so important to tease out for everyone in thinking about your work. Obviously in *Ballet Mécanique for Six Mechanical Sweepers*, you were trying to make that connection to Constructivism. But, I wonder if you could speak more about what Constructivism as a movement has meant to you, just your personal connection to it. What felt interesting to you about that history? Were there particular artists or artworks? Things you read?

MLU: I have to tell you, it's been an ambition of mine for decades to learn a lot, lot, lot more. My knowledge is pretty thin because I think that I took what I wanted.

SJ: That's what I'm asking though. What did you want? What did you take?

MLU: I like Tatlin's tower, the project for the *Monument to the Third International* (1919–20).

SJ: Why do you like it?

MLU: Well, because it's very optimistic. It also looks sort of handmade and even a little shaky and precarious—that it's made by someone who said, "What the hell, we are going to do this!" Like that. Yet, there's a wonderful spiral in it as well, so it has complexity and even a contradiction to this massive revolutionary fervor. I love that.

And also just what I read about mass performances in factories—like, what the hell! You know, "Stop work, let's create something"—that huge love for the people there and faith in them and that what they could create was as valuable as their labor. A sort of spiritual side of Constructivism.

SJ: And that is what you're saying in your text, how you wanted to have the artwork in the space of work, the space of labor, rather than having it on the side or . . .

MLU: I always resisted having the making of the artwork happen outside work, like a hobby or a leisure activity. It had to be real within the work world itself. That's probably the most impractical thing of all my work. I had this notion that it had to happen right at work, that we had to make room as part of work. You know why, because I think that culture can easily become very irreal, unreal. It has to do with power. The job can confer the power to respond to the questions of how you survive, how you make a living. I want the art to be *that* necessary. Culture has to be as necessary as food.

SJ: Right. It does seem worth talking about the mass quality of some of your performances, that so many aspects of your work function on a really large scale. It seems like a lot of artists just don't work that way, on a huge scale of coordination. And it seems like the Constructivist legacy helps or at least gives you permission to do that.

MLU: Absolutely! That is what they were talking about or tried to get the power to talk about: the artist is at the table of creating the whole culture. You know, I have always said that the artist has to be at the decision-making table. I have to tell you, that having also tried to do big permanent work, I mean—it's a whole other subject. But these ballets are what this book is about—better not to go down that "permanent" road. [*Laughter*]

TF: Let me just say one thing about this decision-making table. I went with you once to the sanitation headquarters and there was *that* table in the commissioner's office, that literal table surrounded by about eight guys on each side and one guy at the end. Seventeen men, right? And Mierle was there to say, "We're doing a project in LA, here's the cocurator"— I'm just sort of standing in the back—"and we need a letter from you at this table to that table in LA to make this happen." And that's how it happened. The letter was sent and Los Angeles's municipal workers were enlisted. And that's how you end up with a million pounds of glass and all these recycling trucks driving around the museum. Everybody at that table knew you already and everybody at that table was willing to send a serious letter to that other table to make it happen.

MLU: The letters do make it happen. I'm glad that happened when I did *Vuilniswagendans* (1985) in Rotterdam, which was the first ballet outside of New York City where I was testing my premise that maintenance art is universal work. I can work anywhere, especially if there's a city. Can I cocreate something when I don't speak Dutch? And the way that it happened, the sani-

tation commissioner wrote to the sanitation commissioner in Rotterdam, or in Japan: "You know, she's not crazy, she's worked with us, she's okay."

TF: What about the future of these performances? Even when you recreated the piece in Japan, it was different because Romeo was around, but Juliet had retired.

MLU: And then, actually, Romeo left for another job. We had to get a brand new Romeo and a brand new Juliet and they were phenomenal.

TF: You could recreate one of these ballets, but there would be all these open-ended elements, like the idea is that the artist will go in and sit down with people and find out what they are good at, what they want . . .

MLU: Even what they fantasize about . . .

TF: An essential part of the project is that you're there and part of your genius as an artist is to include all of these different imaginations. I understand how you can get the workers' input, but I don't understand how someone else could make it into a work of art that's still Mierle Ukeles's *Romeo and Juliet*.

MLU: So, part of it is, so what? You know, you have a Pollock painting, and screw it! No one is going to make it again. The only thing is that I can go look at that Pollock painting twenty years down the road and I can't go look at that ballet. So that's like the ephemerality of the . . .

SJ: And an institution can ask to have that painting on loan so somebody else can see it elsewhere.

MLU: Right, so the Pollock does have an afterlife of its own, not dependent on young artists asked to recreate or re-perform it. Let them do their own work. In hoping to have the video documentation have the spirit of the performance, I tried to very hard to pay attention to the video documentation of the ballet that I just did in Japan. But, even though I had a great video team, I couldn't direct what I was seeing for the video also. I had to focus on creating the work with the workers.

TF: But Mierle, I think you're making a mistake.

MLU: You mean because the documentation isn't the work?

TF: It's completely different. You just have to take that material and make a work of art out of it.

MLU: Right, you're completely right. I have been thinking about this a lot. After the moment of the performance has passed, the artist could shift to making a different work that is created in a different time, using the so-called media documentation and even incorporating the memory of the original performance, as a ground plane, and what could emerge is a different work of art, as you say.

SJ: I do think that this question about artworks that expire—and whether they are going to have an afterlife—is important. It seems to me that every artwork has its own parameters for setting up its future. It probably wouldn't be that every single piece that you made, Mierle, would be something that you would want to have recreated in this mode—with Mierle Laderman Ukeles's "operating principles" in circulation. But there might be some that could be conceived or reconceived as a transmission of operating principles, and that might be the work. Meanwhile, other pieces are interesting to watch as documentation. In those cases, the way they will be re-performed will be through their documentation. And there are other models. But I feel like there is not going to be one silver bullet for every artwork, nor one ethical principle for governing the afterlife of an artwork. Each work might provide its own inspiration for what its future can be.

MLU: Well, I think that you're suggesting another level of responsibility, that of the artist to think forward in time. This might be fruitful especially for artists who deal with duration and repetition.

March 19, 2013

227

MIERLE LADERMAN UKELES

After giving birth to her first child in 1968, artist Mierle Laderman Ukeles became a mother/maintenance worker. She had struggled for years to be as free as her avant-garde heroes—Jackson Pollock, Marcel Duchamp, and Mark Rothko—but when she discovered that none of them changed diapers, she fell out of the picture of the avant-garde, where artistic freedom was equated with autonomy. Insisting on surviving as an artist and claiming that art itself must change, she wrote "Manifesto for Maintenance Art 1969!" in a quiet rage in one sitting, which applied equally to the home, all kinds of service work, the urban environment, and the sustainability of the earth itself. She viewed the manifesto as a world vision and a call for revolution for the workers of survival who could, if organized, reshape the world. Still exhibited and taught today, it has become a key document of feminist and social-practice art.

Inspired as well by New York City's "comprehensive plan," whose mission was split into two systems—development and maintenance—Ukeles has created works that collide the two; she understands these systems as the embodiment of opposing human drives of freedom and necessity. Her works seek to test, provoke, expand, and even explode these boundaries, always raising the question, "Is this work necessary?" and then asking, "What does this work do to one's freedom?"

She is madly in love with the public domain and public culture and sees it as *the* area where everyone can be inside the picture. Thus, virtually all her works take place in the public sphere. She asks if we can design modes of survival for a thriving, non-entropic planet that do not crush our personal and civic freedom or silence the individual's voice.

Since 1977, when she became the official, unsalaried Artist-in-Residence at the New York City Department of Sanitation—a position she still holds—Ukeles has created art that deals with the endless maintenance and service work that "keeps the city alive": urban waste flows, recycling, ecology, urban sustainability, and our power to transform degraded land and water into healthy inhabitable public places. One of her best-known projects, *Touch Sanitation* (1977–80), involved facing New York City's 8,500 sanitation workers one at a time, shaking the hand of each, and saying, "Thank you for keeping New York City alive."

Ukeles works in a variety of mediums, creating installations, performances, permanent public art, and media works. From 1983 to 2012 she completed seven "work ballets"—involving workers, trucks, barges, and hundreds of tons of recyclables—in New York City, the Netherlands, Pittsburgh, France, and Japan. The artist tells the story of these ballets in this book.

Ukeles has exhibited internationally, including at the Wadsworth Atheneum, Hartford (1973, 1998); Whitney Museum, New York (1976, 1978, 1985); MoMA PS1, New York (1988, 2008, 2013); Queens Museum, New York (1992, 1995, 2005, 2013, 2014); Los Angeles Museum of Contemporary Art (1995, 1997, 2007, 2012); Tel Aviv Museum (1999); Armory Art Show, New York (2007); Sharjah Biennial 8, United Arab Emirates (2007); Contemporary Jewish Museum, San Francisco (2005, 2008); Smack Mellon, Brooklyn (2010); Wellcome Trust, London (2011); Brooklyn Museum, New York (2012, 2013); Haus der Kunst, Munich (2012); Grazer Kunstverein, Graz (2013); Arnolfini, Bristol (2013); 13th Istanbul Biennial (2013); The Kitchen, New York (2013); Art Institute of Chicago (2013, 2014); Museum of Contemporary Art, Chicago (2013); Institute of Modern Art, Brisbane (2014); Manifesta 10, St. Petersburg (2014); and Marabouparken Art Gallery and Konsthall C, Stockholm (2015). She is represented by Ronald Feldman Fine Arts in New York City.

She has received grants from the National Endowment for the Arts, the New York State Council on the Arts, and Andy Warhol Foundation for the Visual Arts, and fellowships from the John Simon Guggenheim Memorial Foundation, Joan Mitchell Foundation, Anonymous Was a Woman, and the Foundation for Jewish Culture, among others. Her recent teaching includes positions as senior critic in sculpture at Yale University and lecturer at Bard College, UCLA, Harvard Graduate School of Design, Maryland Institute College of Art, Columbia University, Storm King Art Center, and the San Francisco Art Institute. Recent published writing includes "Forgiveness for the Land: Public Offerings Made by All, Redeemed by All," in *Considering Forgiveness* (Vera List Center for Art and Politics, 2009); and "The Power of the Artist & The Power of Art in the Public Domain," in *Creative Time: The Book* (Princeton Architectural Press, 2007).

Ukeles has received honorary doctorates from the Rhode Island School of Design and the Maine College of Art. She received a BA in international relations and history from Barnard College in 1961, and an MA in interrelated arts from New York University in 1974. In 1961 she was appointed member of President John F. Kennedy's delegation to the Independence Celebration of Tanzania, based on her senior thesis.

KARI CONTE is a New York–based curator and writer. Since 2010, she has been the Director of Programs and Exhibitions at the International Studio & Curatorial Program (ISCP). At ISCP, she leads residencies, exhibitions, and public programs in which she collaborates with more than a hundred artists each year. Previously, she worked at Whitechapel Gallery, London, and received an MA in Curating Contemporary Art at the Royal College of Art. She has curated or organized over thirty international exhibitions, site-specific commissions, and performances including contributions to the Aichi Triennale and Performa Biennial. She has given recent talks at institutions including Art in General, Bard College, Creative Time, Goethe-Institut, Independent Curators International (ICI), Ludwig Museum, Purchase College, and Sharjah Art Foundation.

TOM FINKELPEARL is the Commissioner of the New York City Department of Cultural Affairs. In this role he oversees city funding for nonprofit arts organizations across the five boroughs and directs the cultural policy for the City of New York. Prior to his appointment by Mayor Bill de Blasio, Commissioner Finkelpearl served as Executive Director of the Queens Museum for twelve years starting in 2002, overseeing an expansion that doubled the museum's size and positioning the organization as a vibrant center for social engagement in nearby communities. He also held positions at P.S.1 Contemporary Art Center, working on the organization's merger with the Museum of Modern Art, and served as Director of the Department of Cultural Affairs Percent for Art program.

KRIST GRUIJTHUIJSEN is a curator, artistic director of the Grazer Kunstverein in Graz, and course director of the MA Fine Arts Department at the Sandberg Institute in Amsterdam. He is the curator of Mierle Laderman Ukeles's exhibition "Maintenance Art Works 1969–1980," which traveled to the Grazer Kunstverein; Arnolfini, Bristol; Institute of Modern Art, Brisbane; and Marabouparken/Konsthall C in Stockholm. He is the cofounding director (together with Maxine Kopsa) of Kunstverein in Amsterdam and has organized exhibitions and projects at Manifesta 7, Platform Garanti, Istanbul; Artists Space, New York; Museum of Contemporary Art, Belgrade; Swiss Institute, New York; Stedelijk Museum, Amsterdam; Marres, Centre for Contemporary Culture, Maastricht; Project Arts Centre, Dublin; and the Museum of Contemporary Art in Salt Lake City, among others. Gruijthuijsen has produced and edited publications on artists including Doug Ashford, Ben Kinmont, and Lisa Oppenheim, in addition to several others under the umbrella of Kunstverein Publishing.

SHANNON JACKSON is Director of the Arts Research Center and Goldman Professor of Rhetoric and of Theater, Dance, and Performance Studies at the University of California, Berkeley. Jackson's books include *Social Works: Performing Art, Supporting Publics* (2011), *Lines of Activity: Performance, Historiography, and Hull-House Domesticity* (2000), and *Professing Performance: Theatre in the Academy from Philology to Performativity* (2004). Forthcoming from MIT Press is her book about performance and new media that focuses on productions by the Builders Association. Jackson has received numerous awards, including a 2015 John Simon Guggenheim Fellowship and the ATHE Outstanding Book Award. She regularly organizes symposia, public lectures, artist residencies, and community art projects, and is on the board of Cal Performances, the Berkeley Art Museum, and A Blade of Grass.